THE SOCIAL BLACK BELT

Design and Layout by
BRANDFACTORY.COM

Printed in the U.S.A.
www.thesocialblackbelt.com

ACKNOWL- EDGEMENTS

Our deepest gratitude to The Social Black Belt's most consistent and ardent supporter, six-time baseball state champion and Florida High School Athletic Hall of Fame inductee, Coach Craig Faulkner of Venice High School, whose unparalleled leadership inspires greatness in everyone around him, on and off the field. Thank you, Coach, for all you've done for our program and our community.

To Principals Candace Millington, Jack Turgeon, Dr. Steven Covert, David Jones, and Dr. Rachel Shelley; and to Master Chief Jack Sanzalione and all the inspirational teachers and program leaders in Sarasota County who have believed in The Social Black Belt and have allowed us the special opportunity to work by your sides to improve the lives of so many young people: Thank you. Our gratitude for your support cannot be overstated.

To members of the Board of Directors and Advisory Committee, past and present alike, Dr. Jill Scarpellini, Lou Koerner, Gerda Robinson, Harsha Archarya, Amanda Florian, Chris Florand, Jennifer Prosperi,

Barbara Senior, Will Austin, Robert Vedder, Jed Haslam-Walker, Dr. Michael Jaquith, and Michael Marshall: Thank you. Your individual and collective efforts will have more impact in our communities than you will ever know.

Special thanks to Eric Robinson for his financial support, to our editor Hillary Ferrara for her keen eye and generosity of time, to Joe Ulisano for his marketing expertise, and to Martin Pohlmann and Leslie Carol for their exceptional design work. Our program and this book would not be what they are without your help.

Finally, to Dr. Bob Dein, whose generosity of time and resources are exceeded only by his passion for our program: Without your support, neither The Social Black Belt program nor this book would be what they are today, and we are honored to have your leadership and support. Your legacy will live on as the thousands of young people whose mental and emotional health are improved today grow to be the competent and compassionate leaders of tomorrow. A million thanks are not enough.

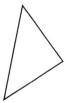

TABLE OF CONTENTS

INTRODUCTION

INTRO - DUCTION

———

When I was young, I used to love watching kung fu and Karate movies, so I frequently asked my mom to sign me up for Karate lessons. Of course, she was afraid I would get hurt—which was probably true—so for a long time she resisted. Eventually, however, she relented and signed me up for a class. I remember being so excited on my way to the class—I couldn't wait to kick butt like Bruce Lee—but when I got there, things did not go as I expected. Not only did I not get to defeat any samurai warriors like I was certain I would, I didn't even get to participate. The sensei explained that I was not ready to participate, so I had to watch the entire class from the sidelines. No broken boards, no death grips, and not one kick, chop, or throw. The worst part, though, was that I was told I would have to wait *two whole weeks* for my *gi*—the traditional uniform worn in Karate. *This*, I felt, was an injustice I could not accept. In the car I told my mom I would not be returning for my second class, and my warrior days were over before they began.

I tell you this story for two reasons. First, I want you to be aware that if we are ever attacked together by evil ninjas in a dark alley, you'd better save yourself. Second, I want you to know that I know what it is like to have a dream and to do absolutely nothing about it. But I also know what it is like to have a dream and to work *really* hard to achieve it, and here, my friends, is how I can help you. I will explain.

Have you ever felt sad or angry, and you weren't sure why? Have you done or said something even though you knew it would get you in trouble? Have you ever worried about things you couldn't control, been disappointed by the actions of your friends and family, or invested a ton of time trying to help someone who didn't want to help themselves? Have you ever been hurt so badly that you feel you will never get over it? Or maybe sometimes you just feel off track or stuck in a rut—like your life is something that *happens* to you instead of something you *actively control*. If you're like the rest of us, the answer to some of these questions is occasionally yes.

But what if you find yourself feeling this way almost all the time—or at least far more often than you would like? Or what if you only feel this way or experience these things sometimes, but can't figure out why? The Social Black Belt can help.

What, exactly, *is* a Social Black Belt, you ask? Well, it's simple. Just as having a black belt in martial arts can protect you physically, having a Social Black Belt can protect you emotionally. Having a Social Black Belt means discovering why you sometimes feel sad, anxious, or angry and, better yet, how to overcome these feelings. It means recognizing and correcting your destructive behaviors and knowing what to worry about and what to let go. It means forming healthy new relationships, repairing damaged ones, and letting go of toxic ones. Having a Social Black Belt means knowing whom to trust and whom to ignore. It means knowing what kind of treatment you should accept from others and what kind you should not. In return, it means knowing how to treat them and, better yet, how to treat yourself. Most importantly, having a Social Black Belt means learning how to process and release the pain of your past, and charting a new path into a brighter future.

Sound too good to be true? Well it's not. Every day I meet lots of interesting people—sometimes just a couple, sometimes hundreds—and I teach them how to use their Black Belts. Some of the people I help are drug addicts. Some are suicidal. Some have been raped or witnessed violence in their homes. And some are just a little sad sometimes and need someone to talk to.

Helping them, then, is crucially important work, and it is no small task. But why do they come to me? Why don't they just talk about their trauma to their plumber or mailman? The answer is simple: I am a clinical psychologist, and it is my *job* to help them. You see, I have spent my entire adult life studying the ways people think and behave and using my professional expertise to help them feel better and improve their lives. Along the way, of course, I have used my decades of training to help *myself,* too, and I feel amazing. Even though I never earned my black belt in Karate (or any other belt, for that matter), I have spent all of my adult life earning my *Social* Black Belt—and I can help you earn yours. But there's a catch.

In martials arts like Taekwondo, Karate, Jiu Jitsu, and others, participants earn belts for different levels of expertise of skills and techniques like blocks, kicks, and throws. But their belts don't represent just their technical abilities—they represent years of hard work, discipline, and dedication. In other words, you can't just sign up for a Karate class, kick a few people, and expect to be handed a belt. I found this out when I was young, but I didn't really learn what it meant until I was much older. The same is true of the Social Black Belt. There is no magic here, no overnight solution. If you want to be happier, healthier, and more emotionally centered, it's going to take some work, but that's okay. You've come to the right place.

Over the course of this book, I will help you on your path to the Social Black Belt. To do so, I will introduce you to Ten Truths that I have learned over the years. I have taught these Truths to thousands of patients with excellent results. In each chapter I will share with you the basic ideas surrounding these truths, stories of patients who have used them to improve their lives, and ways you can use them to improve yours. You will find at the end of each chapter a series of activities related to these truths. I encourage you, then, not just to read the chapters, but to do the exercises as well. The exercises may be painful at times, and that's okay. Just as you can't earn a black belt in Karate by watching a couple Bruce Lee movies and going to one class, you can't earn a Social Black Belt and, more importantly, the happiness it provides you, without wrestling with some emotional discomfort along the way. But I am here to guide you, and I promise you will be stronger in the end. Welcome to the Social Black Belt.

Let's begin.

TRUTH N°1

TRUTH N° 1

You Don't Have to be Confused by Your Feelings Anymore

Imagine if you could know your emotions as well as you know your thoughts. Consider what your life would be like if you could control your feelings rather than allowing them to control you. Instead of finding yourself overcome by sadness, you would be able to connect this feeling to a specific source and address it. Instead of getting angry or upset and yelling at your parents or your boyfriend or girlfriend, you would be alert for when you are about to blow up and could take steps to prevent it. You could prevent your negative feelings from disrupting you and could experience your positive emotions fully. Is this possible? Not only is it possible, but anyone can do it. Anyone who is willing to put in a little bit of work, that is. And the best part? It doesn't require years of therapy or professional training. All it takes is a desire to change, a willingness to undertake the process, an attitude of openness and honesty with yourself, and the discipline to apply what you have learned about yourself to your future behaviors. By understanding the sources, meanings, and physiology of your feelings—in other words, your body's physical reactions to your emotional states—you can exercise more power and control over them and lead a happier and more fulfilling life.

Think about Tyler, who has a horrible temper. He blows up at the smallest annoyance. Last summer, Tyler's girlfriend broke up with him because he screamed at her repeatedly in public; last winter, he was kicked off the basketball team for punching one of his teammates; and just this week he was suspended from school for cursing at his teacher and flipping his desk. At age 16, Tyler has already given up on changing and has accepted his anger. He doesn't really understand why he becomes so furious, and he wishes he could do something about it, but he figures, *I guess that's just the way I am.* Tyler doesn't have to be this way. He can change. If Tyler can figure out the source of his anger and the triggers that unleash it, he has an excellent chance of controlling it and preventing it from doing any more damage in his life. And, quite possibly, by controlling his emotions, Tyler might be able to undo at least some of the damage his anger has already caused.

Forget Tyler for a moment, and let's think about your cell phone. The manufacturer believes that your user experience will be significantly better if you know how the cell phone works, so the company provides a user's manual explaining its various functions. You may not read every word on every page. You've probably already learned a lot about your new phone from using previous models or other types of cell phones, but you're curious about the new, unfamiliar features and how they function. Maybe it's your first time owning a phone with facial recognition technology, for example, so you read the manual for set up instructions. Maybe the first time you try to set it up, you don't succeed, so you read the instructions again and then you've got it. Knowing how to set up your new phone's facial recognition features does not automatically make you a professional cell phone designer or engineer, but it does allow you to use these features to better operate your new cell phone going forward. In much the same way, you don't need a psychologist's understanding of emotions to control them, but learning even one aspect of how they function in your life can be tremendously useful.

In his classic psychology book, *The Road Less Traveled*, [1] Dr. M. Scott Peck argues that emotions are slaves, and we are their masters. In other words, we control our emotions, they don't control us. If you are like most teenagers, this is not how you would describe your relationship with them. But, there's good news. You *can* be the master of your emotions, and you don't need to be a psychologist to understand how to do this. Let's take the first step by introducing five simple secrets about emotions:

1. All Your Emotions Are Statements About You

2. Your Emotions Are Usually the Result of Your Thoughts, Attitudes, and Perceptions

3. You Are Most Emotional About the Things in Which You Have the Greatest Investment, Especially When Those Investments Are Threatened

4. Your Emotions Communicate How You Perceive Reality

5. Emotions Express Themselves in Three Distinct Forms

Now let's discuss these five pieces of psychological wisdom one at a time.

1. All Your Emotions Are Statements About You

Your emotions can be traced back to the way you process reality. As a psychologist who treats clients who have experienced trauma and abuse, I often hear stories about the sexual abuse of children by adult caretakers—friends, parents, teachers. And though I've never experienced these kinds of abuses personally, I still undergo emotional and physiological changes when I listen to these patients graphically describe the ways in which they were violated as children. I grit my teeth and clench my fists. My heart rate increases. In other words, I become *angry*. But this anger is not a reflection of my personal experiences; it is a reflection of who I *am*. By this I do not mean that I am an angry *person*; I mean that I *become* angry when I perceive that adults have misused their power, violated the trust placed in them, and abused innocent children in their care. This reaction, then, is a statement about my thoughts and beliefs about abuse and a reflection of my values, both as a psychologist and as an individual.

A retired teacher, Mrs. Washington, became a client when she was nearly 80. A kind, gentle woman with a quick smile and a warm laugh, she told stories of more than 30 years of teaching high school science in the inner city. Mrs. Washington had a habit of describing her students—her babies, as she called them—as precious, beautiful, and lovely. "She was a precious baby." "He was a lovely boy." Consider why she used these words. Was it because every student she spoke of was as "precious" and "lovely" as Mrs. Washington believed? Possibly. But more likely, her use of these words says more about her than it does about her students. It suggests that Mrs. Washington herself was warm, compassionate, and loving.

Now imagine Jeff, who never has a kind word to say to or about anyone. "He's a jerk." "She's a loser." Just as Mrs. Washington's words of kindness suggest that she, herself, is kind, so, too, do Jeff's frequently rude or insulting words suggest a great deal about him. I bet you know a Mrs. Washington and a Jeff, but the question is: How do *you* describe others? And what does this say about *you*?

Now consider how you feel when you're driving and how this mindset influences your emotions and behaviors. Maybe behind the wheel you are like driver A: hypercautious, inclined to obey every traffic law, always yielding to other vehicles to avoid an accident. Perhaps you're at the other end of the spectrum, like person B: navigating the roads like you're a racecar driver, speeding constantly and weaving in and out of traffic. Or perhaps, like driver C, you're one of those people who feels entitled, like the road is yours and everyone else is in your way, angry when people cut you off or when people in front of you drive too slowly. Now think about how you feel and act when you approach a yellow light. If you're driver A, you feel caution and brake for safety. If you're driver B, you feel the rush of a challenge and press the gas. And if you're driver C, you feel frustration and anger and punch the wheel when you stop at the light, cursing at it the whole time. In this sense, the light literally signals your emotions. You can use these signals to understand how your mindset impacts your emotions and how these emotions impact your behavior.

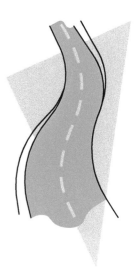

The bottom line: your emotions are reflections of you, not external stimuli. And, not everyone reacts to every situation the same way. So while you can't always control what happens to you, you *can* control how you react to it. Just as you have the power to choose to be happy, you have the power to choose how you will react next time you perceive that you have been offended, wronged, or violated in some way. Next time you feel yourself becoming angry, choose patience. Next time you feel yourself becoming sad, choose positive thinking. You'll like the results.

2. Your Emotions Are Usually the Result of Your Thoughts, Attitudes, and Perceptions

A man lies fast asleep on a city sidewalk, half in, half out of a cardboard box. His worn face rests on the arm of his dirty shirt. Drool falls onto his sleeve. Four pedestrians walk by. The first one notices the sleeping man's pitiful condition but looks away. *I didn't see anything,* he thinks, as he continues his morning walk without another thought of the man on the sidewalk. The second pedestrian spots the man in her peripheral vision and says to herself, *That man could have been me back in my partying days. I'm so grateful I got sober.* Then she offers the man a silent prayer as she continues her walk to work. The third pedestrian has a far different response to the sleeping man; he goes on an inner tirade, thinking, *It's lazy, good-for-nothing bums like him that lie around all day and sleep on the street who are bringing this country down. Here I am working my butt off to make an honest living, and my tax dollars are being used to support people like him. Doesn't he have any pride?* The fourth passerby looks in horror when she first sees the sleeping man. *Oh, that poor man,* she thinks, as she stoops by the side of the unfortunate man. She checks to see if the man is alive, wondering if the elements overcame him and what she can do to help. Finally, she decides to let the man sleep as she gently places a $20 bill in his shirt pocket. As she goes about her day, she thinks frequently about the sleeping man, a profoundly sad image permanently etched in her memory, a painful reminder of the plight of the less fortunate.

Each of these passersby thinks differently about—and thus has a different reaction to—the homeless man because each has a different attitude about homelessness in general. One man thinks homeless people are to be ignored, so that's what he does. A woman is grateful she did not succumb to such a lifestyle, so she reacts with gratitude, and so on. Just remember: your thoughts and attitudes about people and issues will determine your emotional reaction to them, so next time you become emotional about something, examine your thoughts and attitude to help you gain control over your emotions.

Taken another way, consider that your emotions are based on your *perceptions* of reality, not on reality itself. The way you perceive the world leads to your emotional reaction, and sometimes we react to what we *think* we see, not to what is actually happening. Let's take a look at a recent situation involving Kim, Desmond, and Porsha.

Kim and Desmond have been dating for about six months. At the end of last school year, Kim broke up with Tommy because she found out he had been cheating on her with her best friend Julie. This experience left Kim devastated, because not only had she been hurt and embarrassed—it seemed everyone knew but her—but she lost both her boyfriend and her best friend at the same time. So when Desmond sat next to Kim in first period English earlier this year and began to show his interest in her, Kim was naturally a bit hesitant. But Desmond was sweet and charming—not to mention really cute—so eventually Kim let down her guard and decided to give him a chance.

Until recently, everything had been going really well between Desmond and Kim, but lately Kim has started to suspect that something has been going on between Desmond and her new best friend, Porsha. Last week all three were sitting together on the couch, Kim in the middle, and Desmond and Porsha on either side of her, watching a movie together at Porsha's house. About halfway through the movie, Kim stepped out to take a call from her mom, but when she went back inside, Porsha and Desmond were sitting right next to each other, whispering something Kim couldn't hear. When they saw Kim, Desmond and Porsha immediately stopped talking and moved away from each other, visibly embarrassed and unable to explain what they were talking about when Kim asked. And just the other day Kim was coming down the steps from her science lab to meet Desmond at his locker, and she once again saw them whispering to each other and standing a little too close together for comfort. When Kim came upon them by surprise, Porsha became flustered and left in a hurry.

But all Kim's suspicions came to a head yesterday morning in Mrs. Sweitzer's English class. Bored by yet another lecture on the proper use of the semicolon, Desmond raised his hand and asked to use the bathroom, leaving his cell phone on his desk as he left. While he was gone, he got a text. Bored, and maybe a little curious, Kim looked over to see who it was, and to her surprise, it was Porsha! "I can't wait until tonight...," the text read. Kim was angry—furious, even—but most of all she was hurt. How could this have happened to her again? How could she have been so stupid? Just then Desmond returned from the bathroom, and, unable to contain her emotions, Kim left class in tears. When Desmond looked at the text on his phone, he knew Kim must have seen it. All day Desmond tried to talk to Kim, but she avoided him in the halls and ignored his texts. When Porsha tried to approach her in the hall, Kim cursed at her and walked away as Porsha called after her.

After school Kim went home and cried for an hour. She couldn't believe that she had caught yet another boyfriend cheating with yet another best friend. Determined not to be made a fool, Kim texted Desmond that it was over. Desmond begged for a chance to explain, but Kim would hear none of it. She told him she wanted to pick up her math textbook and the sweater she had left at his place the weekend before. He replied that he would be home at seven, and then she blocked his number. Heading to Desmond's later that evening, Kim rehearsed all the choice words she would say to him when she got there, becoming angrier by the minute. She thought she might even slap him just for good measure. When she arrived, Desmond's parents' car was in the driveway, and the porch light was on, but all the lights in the house were off. "I want my stuff back, Desmond," was all Kim could say when Desmond came to the door. "All right," he replied. "Come on in while I run up to grab it." Kim entered the house and stood alone in the darkened foyer as Desmond walked away. Moments later, every light in the house came on suddenly and 25 people screamed, "SURPRISE!!!" In front of Kim stood Desmond and Porsha, beaming under a giant banner that read, "Happy Birthday Kimmy! We Love You!"

Kim's mistake was understandable. Because she had been betrayed before, Kim was primed to believe that it was happening again, and her false perceptions impacted how she felt. We've all reacted to something only to discover later that our feelings were impacted by a perception of reality that was inaccurate or misguided. The point: our *perceptions*, not reality itself, impact our emotions, so next time you are about to react to a situation, first be sure your misguided perceptions aren't clouding your judgement.

3. You Are Most Emotional About the Things in Which You have the Greatest Investment, Especially When Those Investments are Threatened

Feelings sometimes describe who you are—happy kid, cranky man, nervous mother—but they also indicate what you care about. The people and things you care most about—your boyfriend, your parents, the success of your cross-country team—are known as investments, and your investments are where you put your emotional energy. If you feel emotions for someone or something, you are invested. If you feel strongly, you are very invested. Here's an example:

Who do you want to win the upcoming mayoral election in Phoenix, Arizona? Unless you happen to live there, you probably don't care, and since you don't care, you won't have an emotional reaction to the results. Why? Because without investment, there will be no emotional output. Now think about who you want to win Class President this year, or Homecoming King, or Team Captain of your volleyball team. Chances are you probably care about these things a whole lot more than you care about who becomes mayor of Phoenix, even though they are actually far less important, because you are invested in their outcomes. The people involved are your friends, and the environment is your school, so you have an emotional investment in the results.

Using emotion as a way of determining what's important to you can help you make important life decisions. If you don't feel an emotional reaction to something, then it probably isn't that important to you. If you feel yourself reacting strongly, however, then you are probably much more heavily invested, even if at first you did not realize it. Naturally, we react most strongly when our investments are at risk. For example, if you found out that an ice cream parlor in the next town over was going out of business, you probably wouldn't care a whole lot, but if that same ice cream parlor had been in your family for four generations, is currently owned by your parents, and was to be passed on to you when you graduated college, then your reaction would likely be very strong. It is important to understand that the people and things in which you are most heavily invested have the greatest power over how you feel. So assess what matters to you, and control your emotions when threats to these investments arise, as they inevitably will. Bad things will happen; how you react to them is up to you.

One final point about investments: your emotional investments in people and things change constantly. Things you used to care about may mean little to you now, and things you used to care little for in the past may grow to mean a great deal to you over time. Your change in emotional output, one way or the other, is a sign that something's level of importance to you is changing.

4. Your Emotions Communicate How You Perceive Reality

Think of your emotions as inner messengers that provide information about how you perceive reality. Unfortunately, you may sometimes misinterpret those messages or feel too emotional to understand what they are telling you. For example, we've all been sad or angry, but what do these emotions actually *mean*, and what might they be telling us about ourselves? To get a better understanding, let's look at some possible ways to interpret some of the most common emotional responses.

ANXIETY

Anxiety is a nervous feeling that sometimes includes an increased heart rate, upset stomach, excessive sweating, shallow breathing, difficulty sleeping, and many other symptoms. It's a relatively common feeling that most people have experienced at one time or another. Sometimes you can identify its source—a speech you have to give in French next period, or the championship game against your school's biggest rival later today, for example—but sometimes it's a vague feeling whose root cause is harder to identify. Even when you know the source of your anxiety, however, the emotional message is incomplete, and it's important to understand what this emotion is telling you.

In order to gain a full understanding of your anxiety, it will help to view it as your body's way of reacting when something you care about—in other words, something you are invested in—is threatened. For example, let's say you have a goal to get into a specific college to study in their chemistry department, but math is not your strongest subject. You've always done your homework, gone to tutoring, and watched all the tutorials on YouTube, but despite your best efforts, you've never managed to get better than a B- in your classes. Nevertheless, you love working with chemicals in the lab and are determined that your weakness in math won't prevent you from reaching your goal. Like most colleges, the one you are trying to get into is very competitive. They only take the best and most qualified candidates, so knowing you might not be accepted if you don't score well on the math section of the SAT tomorrow has been upsetting your stomach and keeping you up every night for the past week. In this scenario, you have an investment (you really want to study chemistry at a particular college), and there is a threat to that investment (a poor SAT score may prevent your acceptance). Thus, your anxiety is a sign that something you care about may be threatened. Examining anxiety from this perspective is helpful because it gives you the information you need to address its root cause, and if you address the root cause effectively, you are more likely to be relieved of your negative feelings.

But *how*, exactly, do you address the sources of your anxiety? Well, head on, of course. If you're nervous about flying, book a flight. If you're anxious about public speaking, give a speech. If you've been debating with yourself whether to try out for the baseball team, just do it. And if you're worried about having low SAT scores, go to tutoring, study, and take lots of practice tests. The alternative is to try to ignore these nervous feelings by avoiding the situations that produce them, but doing so will likely only prolong these anxious feelings and guarantee that they surface again as soon as similar situations arise, which they will.

SADNESS

With sadness, the message is somewhat different. In this case, instead of perceiving a *threat* to something we care about, we perceive its *loss*. The death of a loved one, a friend's moving away, or the breakup of a relationship can all create feelings of sadness. Sadness is something we all have experienced, but it is not the same as major depression, which is a clinical diagnosis marked by at least two weeks of symptoms such as sadness, insomnia, feelings of hopelessness and/or worthlessness, apathy, changes in appetite, and other symptoms. While sadness can be *part* of clinical depression, by itself it is a normal human emotion. As long as it diminishes over time, you're not depressed. If you believe you are depressed, however, you should tell someone you trust—a teacher, a parent, or a guidance counselor, perhaps—so you can get the help that you need.

Sometimes you may not understand why you're sad. You may think it has something to do with bad weather, for example. And sometimes you don't want to admit that you're sad. Maybe you don't want to admit that your ex's cheating has hurt you. But the key to overcoming sadness is to identify what thing of value you have lost and to come to terms with it in a healthy way. It's okay to say a tearful goodbye to your grandmother or favorite pet and mourn for some time. But then spend time with friends or take up a new hobby. Just understand that the sooner you understand why you're sad and make an effort to come to terms with your loss, the sooner you will recover from your negative feelings.

GUILT

Two friends walk into a convenience store together. Each takes a candy bar and leaves without paying. One boy enjoys the sweet taste of chocolate, thinking nothing of how he came to possess it, while the other tosses his candy bar in the trash can and loses sleep for a month over his illegal act. So why does one boy feel nothing while the other is overcome with guilt? Because we do not feel guilty when we do something wrong; we feel guilty when we *think* we have done something wrong or have violated our moral code in some way. Both boys did something wrong, committed a crime, in fact, but while the first boy sees nothing wrong with his act (he wanted a candy bar but didn't have any money, so he took it), the second boy was taught from a young age that it is wrong to take what does not belong to you. Hence, one boy feels a sugar high, while the other feels terrible guilt.

Here's another example. Two men are fishing on a beautiful Sunday morning. One man is enjoying the calm waters and the blue skies, while the other is plagued with an irritating sense of guilt. Surely fishing is not an immoral act, so why does the second man feel guilty? You see, he was raised in a religious family who taught him that one must be in church on Sunday mornings. While he enjoys fishing and sees nothing inherently wrong with doing it, he believes that fishing instead of going to church is morally wrong, so he feels guilty. Again, it is not the act committed that makes one experience guilt; it is the perception that you have violated your moral code that causes that negative feeling.

While no one particularly likes to experience guilty feelings, guilt is helpful because it can help you examine the validity of your moral code. The boy who felt guilty about stealing the candy bar should use that experience to determine that his feelings are valid, that stealing is wrong, and that he should never do it again. The man who feels guilt about fishing, however, might reach one of two conclusions after examining his feelings. If he determines that, yes, his skipping church to fish is morally wrong, then he should change his behavior and be in the front row next week. If he determines that his belief that he must go to church on Sundays is a result of living by his *parents'* moral code rather than his own and that he can go to church another day of the week, or even not at all, then he should relieve himself of his guilty feelings and bait another hook.

In order to feel guilty and make choices according to your moral standards, you must first learn the difference between right and wrong. You must also understand that each person has different beliefs about what constitutes right and wrong behavior. Some people are guilt sponges, constantly feeling weighed down by the perception that they have done something wrong, while others feel no guilt despite committing horrible acts. Again, it is not your behavior that causes you to feel guilty, but the perception that the behavior runs counter to your moral code.

Next time you experience feelings of guilt, examine your moral code. If you realize that you have, in fact, violated it in some way, resolve to do better next time to avoid the nagging feeling. If, however, you determine that you have not violated your moral code and that your feelings of guilt are unwarranted, come to terms with this revelation by believing that you have, in fact, made a right choice, so there is no reason to feel bad about it. Then, continue with that behavior, knowing you are in the right until the guilt eventually subsides.

PANIC

Some people compare panic attacks to the sensation of dying and/or having a heart attack. They describe feelings of tightness in their chest, racing heart, rapid and shallow breathing, weak knees, upset stomach, and an intense need to escape from some place or experience.

Panic attacks (also known as anxiety attacks) are far more intense than the generalized feelings of nervousness or anxiety described earlier and are a common problem in society, affecting many people. While most people experience anxiety at one time or another, panic disorder is defined by having at least two or three panic attacks per month and/or being preoccupied with thoughts of having them. That means some people experience panic attacks at the thought of having panic attacks. And although some people require medication to deal with panic attacks, many people can control this powerful emotion when they understand these feelings are simply a message that they feel trapped or out of control, and try to deal effectively with these feelings. You can do the same.

Take Sabrina, for instance, who had never experienced a panic attack until she went scuba diving with her parents during a family vacation in Mexico. At first, Sabrina loved the experience—the calm quiet of the waves above, the vibrant colors of the exotic fish—but then her scuba guide took her and her parents into an underwater cave. It wasn't so much what Sabrina found there that made her panic; it was what she didn't find—the exit. Or take Brandon, who experienced his first panic attack during a routine medical procedure. The week before his attack, Brandon was tackled especially hard during a high school football game and had been experiencing severe pain in his back. His mother took him to the doctor to have an MRI of his back taken, and while Brandon was enclosed in the small tube-like machine, perfectly still and alone in the room, he panicked.

Feeling trapped is not based solely on physical circumstances, however. Sometimes people report feeling trapped by bad relationships, dead-end jobs, or other life situations that can cause panic. Take Stephen, for example, who was accepted by a top university near the Gulf of Mexico to study marine biology. However, Tanya, Stephen's girlfriend since eighth grade, has chosen to attend her top choice school in St. Louis. Stephen has been agonizing for months over whether to study marine biology near the water or follow his girlfriend to the Midwest. To make matters worse, Stephen's mother has been battling cancer for the past 18 months, and she really needs his help at home caring for his two younger siblings. With the deadline for accepting his school's offer of admission just two weeks away, Stephen, feeling trapped and unsure what to do, had a panic attack at school.

Understanding what causes panic attacks can help reduce their frequency, intensity, or duration, and can sometimes stop them altogether. It may be helpful to think of panic attacks not as completely random or simply resulting from too much stress, but as a sign that something is making you feel trapped. By recognizing that much of what you are feeling may be the result of perception rather than reality, that the condition is temporary, and that it poses no serious risk, you will be much better equipped to confront the source of the panic attack. Simply avoiding problems in hopes that you will avoid panic attacks, however, proves to be a much less effective way of dealing with your emotional chaos. Escapist behavior may offer short-term relief, but if the root cause of panic attacks is not properly dealt with, they will return because the core emotional message has been ignored.

ANGER

Think about who angers you the most and why. Is it your mom because she won't stop nagging you to clean your room? Is it your little brother because he won't stop going through your stuff when you're not home? Is it your boyfriend because he keeps ditching you for his guy friends? On the surface, anger may seem simple enough to understand, but what is essential to understand, and what is often overlooked, is that anger is your mind's way of telling you that you perceive that you have been violated in some way or that your expectations have not been met. You expected a raise at work but didn't get one. You expected your girlfriend to show up on time, but she didn't.

To become angry sometimes is completely normal, but it becomes counterproductive, and potentially harmful, when its frequency, intensity, or duration are beyond the norm. For example, if you have constant temper tantrums, are verbally or physically abusive, or are furious for hours instead of minutes, these may be signs that you have difficulty dealing with anger.

Typically, people who are overly angry make excuses for their behavior. They blame their outbursts on everyone or everything but themselves, but what they fail to realize is that, like with all other emotions, the real source of their anger is internal, not external. When they perceive that a violation has occurred—a friend cheated in a video game or told a secret she promised to keep—they become enraged. But it doesn't have to be this way.

Trying to manage your anger when you're already at the boiling point is an ineffective way to handle this powerful emotion. Instead, it's much more effective to try to understand *why* you become angry and learn to think differently about the cause. It is a fact of life that sometimes people will do things to you that you simply don't like. But when you realize that these violations often cannot be avoided, are a reflection of the violator and not you, and are unworthy of the emotional tumult you experience during your bouts of rage, you may be less inclined to overreact when someone or something does not turn out the way you expected it to.

Other emotions exist besides these five, but the goal is to always try to understand that emotions arise based on perceptions of reality. Recognizing this may be difficult in the heat of the moment, but when you ignore the role that perception plays and focus on emotions rather than root causes, you may act in ways that are harmful to yourself and others.

5. Emotions Express Themselves in Three Distinct Forms

Emotions are three-headed creatures, and if you are to fully understand them, you need to consider three important aspects:

 How You're Feeling

 How Your Feelings Impact Your Body

 How You Behave in Response

First, how each person feels is a reflection of each person's individual and personal experience of the world, and no two people experience the world in the same way. For example, you and your boyfriend see the same romantic movie together. You love the movie and cry when the two separated lovers reunite at the end. He rolls his eyes and complains the whole time. You say the movie was beautiful; he says it was stupid. Even if someone is your best friend, your boyfriend, or your twin sister, you simply cannot expect others to feel the same way as you do. You may share common feelings with these people sometimes, but your relationships will be much better the sooner you understand that people's feelings are their own, and they are expressed in different ways.

Second, your emotions can be explained physiologically. Physiology refers to the ways your body reacts when you are feeling particular emotions. For example, when

you are angry, you may clench your fists or pace the room. When you are nervous, you may sweat or tremble. Emotions, then, are more than just a state of mind; they involve a series of complex physical reactions that start in the brain and produce a physical response, so it is important to recognize that your emotional state can impact your physical one. For example, high stress can result in sexual difficulties for men, anger has been associated with heart disease and some forms of cancer, and grief and unresolved sadness may lead to problems in the immune system, making it more difficult for the body to fend off illness. Use your body as a sophisticated warning system. If you're feeling sluggish, if your stomach has been upset for some time, or if you have frequent headaches, consider the possibility that your body is telling you something about your emotional state. If you can identify the cause of your emotional distress and confront it proactively, your physical symptoms will likely disappear as well.

Third, your emotions drive certain behaviors. When you laugh, yell, cry, smile, make sarcastic remarks, or become aggressive, these behaviors are the consequences of emotions. Understanding behavior, then, is key to understanding feelings. Behavior communicates how you feel and allows you to release your emotions. If you are bursting with happiness, you may want to laugh, sing, or do a little dance. When you are sad, you may need to cry. When you are angry, you may want to scream into a pillow. Not only do these behaviors help relieve certain emotional pressures, they let others know exactly how you're feeling on the inside. If you try to separate your emotions from your behaviors—in other words, if you don't act the way you feel—you probably won't feel very good. It's not enough just to *say* that you're happy or sad; it is important, too, to be able to express your emotions through appropriate behavior.

To understand and experience your emotions fully, it is important to understand their mental, physical, and behavioral manifestations. If you can appreciate the individual nature of feelings, recognize their physical aspects, and express them through appropriate behavior, you will function much more effectively in the world and feel a whole lot better about yourself. We will discuss how to control these behaviors in the next chapter.

---

[1]   Peck, M. Scott. *The Road Less Traveled.*
New York: Simon and Schuster, 1978.

FORGIVE

Forgive...

everyone and everything. The fewer grudges you carry around with you, the lighter you will feel.

Be Optimistic...

A positive outlook will lead you to positive outcomes.

Build Relationships...

founded on love. If you surround yourself with people you love and who love you in return, you will be happier and feel more secure.

Be Grateful...

for all the good things in life, and express your thanks to others. An attitude of gratitude will help you maintain perspective when life throws you curveballs.

Invest...

your time and energy in things that matter. Having purpose and passion will give you a reason to be your best self every day.

Volunteer...

Helping people builds self-confidence, pride, and a sense of belonging to a community; and when others know you are there for them, they are more likely to be there for you when the time comes.

Exercise Often and Eat Well...

Be active, be fit. A healthy body helps support a healthy mind. Frequent vigorous exercise and a healthy diet can improve your happiness and extend your life significantly.

EXERCISES

The first Truth is all about getting to know your emotions. We've tried to take the mystery out of common emotions like fear, anger, and sadness, and we hope you now have a much better understanding of why you feel the way you do and what these feelings mean. To help you apply this learning to your life, we've created the following four exercises.

20 Questions:
How Did You Feel When...?

This exercise is designed to help you get in touch with your full range of emotions. You may not realize how different your emotions can be from one another, so the prompts here will make you aware of this. The prompts refer to events that occurred in your past, so if a given prompt is not relevant—for example, if you've never experienced the death of a pet—then feel free to change the wording slightly, like this: How *would* you feel *if* your pet died?

1.   When my best friend moved away/When I moved away from my best friend, I felt

_____

_____

2.   When I earned my highest test score, I felt

_____

_____

3.   When my dog/cat/pet passed away, I felt

_____

_____

4.   When my parents fought, I felt

_____

_____

5. When I was falsely accused of something I didn't do, I felt

_____

_____

6. When a friend shared a secret of mine, I felt

_____

_____

7. When the other students wouldn't let me join in, I felt

_____

_____

8. When I got my first job, I felt

_____

_____

9. When my father/mother was drunk when my friends came over, I felt

_____

_____

10. When I vacationed at my favorite place, I felt

_____

_____

11. When someone threatened to harm me, I felt

_____

_____

12. When someone I know spread rumors about me, I felt

_____

_____

13. When my family and friends took care of me when I was sick, I felt

_____

_____

14. When my parent(s) broke a promise to me, I felt

_____

_____

15. When my parent(s) compared me to my sibling/someone else's child, I felt

_____

_____

16. When no one picked me to be on their team, I felt

_____

_____

17. When all my hard work paid off, I felt

_____

_____

18. When I failed the test after studying really hard, I felt

_____

_____

19. When I couldn't stop thinking bad thoughts, I felt

_____

_____

20. When I/my team won the game, I felt

_____

_____

2 What Causes You to Feel That Way?

Understanding your feelings means digging below the surface to identify the root causes of those feelings. Here, we'd like you to finish the prompt with a specific event, situation, or relationship that produces the following feelings.

1. I feel happy when _____

_____

2. I feel sad when _____

_____

3. I feel embarrassed when _____

_____

4. I feel nervous when _____

_____

5. I feel jealous when _____

_____

6. I feel upset when _____

_____

7. I feel confused when _____

_____

8. I feel loved when _____

_____

9. I feel proud when _____

_____

10. I feel irritated when _____

_____

③ Getting to the Bottom of Anger

Anger is always a secondary emotion. It is the result of something happening that you wish had not happened or something not happening that you wish had. Here, rather than dwelling on the negative emotion of anger, try to identify the root cause by finishing the prompt with people or situations that have caused you to feel angry recently.

1. I am angry because _____

_____

2. I get frustrated when _____

_____

3. I can't believe that you _____

_____

Your Top Five Investments

In the chart below, describe the five people or things you are most invested in—in other words, what you care about the most. Then describe the biggest threat to that investment you can imagine. For example, your investment might be your three-year relationship with your boyfriend, and the biggest threat to that investment might be his breaking up with you or your moving to another state. This exercise will help you become clear on what really matters to you and what "unknowns" might be making you feel most anxious.

	INVESTMENT	THREAT
1.		
2.		
3.		
4.		
5.		

TRUTH N° 2

You Can Control Your Compulsive Behaviors if You Change Your Thoughts and Address Your Problems

Now that you have become aware of our previous Truth that emotions can be understood and even controlled, you may wonder whether it's really possible to change the behaviors these emotions produce. Think about what you do when you feel terribly sad or incredibly angry. If you're deeply sad, you may sit around and watch sappy movies or listen to melancholic music. If you're very angry, you may verbally or physically abuse people you care about. Or you may adopt behaviors that are self-destructive, like running away or cutting yourself. You know these behaviors are counterproductive and harmful—and you may even want to stop them—but the emotions that produce them are so powerful that they seem to have a hold over you, creating a pattern of behavior that becomes predictable, dangerous, and compulsive.

Many of us have compulsions. These are behaviors that we feel compelled, or strongly urged, to do, even when we know they are bad for us. Some people drink too much when they're sad. Some smoke when they're anxious. Others have meltdowns when they're angry, or cheat or flirt with other girls when they're lonely. These compulsive behaviors can take many forms, but they have one thing in common: They're always triggered by an intense emotional state.

Take Angie, for example. She's 22, recently married with a 3-year-old son. At 7, she was abandoned when her parents went to prison, and she spent the next several years suffering physical and sexual abuse at the hands of the uncle who took her in. As a result of these experiences, Angie has always felt ashamed, frightened, and vulnerable to being abandoned by anyone, and hurt by men in particular. These feelings have caused lots of problems in Angie's life, including in her relationship with her husband and her effec-tiveness as a parent. To deal with these intense feelings, Angie chose a compulsive behavior as a form of self-medication. Specifically, Angie became a compulsive eater. If she feels rejected by her husband, or if her child defies her, she seeks comfort in a package of cookies. If her male boss criticizes her work performance, she gets together with her best friends, Ben and Jerry. Comfort foods console Angie when she feels worthless, ineffectual, or unloved. But they don't solve her problems.

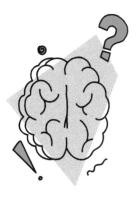

We will return to Angie's story a bit later. For now, recognize that it is possible to escape the cycle of compulsive behavior. Fortunately, obsessions and anxiety are not permanent conditions. They may flood your mind with troubling thoughts, but they don't have to control your behaviors. In fact, when you grasp what emotions are producing these behaviors and how they are causing you to act in this way, you can learn to control them by using your Social Black Belt.

Compulsive Behaviors: Short-term Relief for Long-term Pain

When you act compulsively, you engage in activities that change your emotional state, seemingly for the better, but they produce significant problems in the long run. When you watch TV or play video games compulsively, for example, you may relieve the immediate anxiety you're suffering from by escaping into virtual worlds, but in the long term, this compulsive behavior may prevent you from dealing with the real source of your anxiety. You may temporarily avoid the science project you've been putting off or that weird talk you need to have with your mom, but avoiding these things does not make them go away. Additionally, you may be adding a new problem to your list when you spend too many hours seated in front of the TV and you begin to grow out of shape.

In some people there exists a driving force so powerful that it causes them to engage in behaviors that have serious negative consequences. Angie has become psychologically, and probably physically, addicted to food. When things go bad, she gives herself an emotional fix, a temporary release from the pain she feels, but mostly she just causes more harm in the end. If you learn how these compulsions function and which emotions trigger them, you can prevent engaging in compulsive behaviors by addressing the real causes of your emotional distress.

Consider that compulsive behaviors:

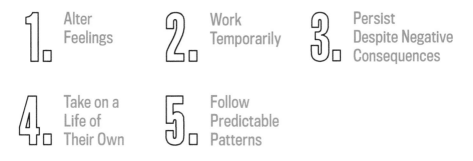

1. Alter Feelings

2. Work Temporarily

3. Persist Despite Negative Consequences

4. Take on a Life of Their Own

5. Follow Predictable Patterns

Let's examine these ideas one at a time.

1. Compulsive Behaviors Alter Feelings

Sometimes compulsive behaviors help you feel something you want to feel. Other times they stop you from feeling what you don't want to feel. People who bite their fingernails know it's a gross habit, but they do it because it alleviates anxiety. People who drink excessively know drinking is dangerous, but the buzz makes them temporarily forget their problems. People engage in compulsive behaviors—drugs, alcohol, sex, shopping, gambling—for countless reasons: problems at work, feeling ignored in a relationship, dealing with trauma—but the ultimate reason people engage in compulsive behaviors is they don't like how they feel, they want to feel differently, and they know compulsive behaviors alter feelings.

2. Compulsive Behaviors Work Temporarily

I have yet to meet a patient who smokes banana peels compulsively. Perhaps some people have tried it as a joke or out of curiosity, but why aren't large numbers of people all over the world smoking banana peels like addicts? Because it doesn't work. We do not get high off smoking banana peels, and they do not help us forget our problems. Marijuana, on the other hand, like Molly, methamphetamine, and many other drugs, is highly effective at providing intense highs and temporary escapes from reality. People use drugs—and not banana peels—because they work, and people repeat behaviors that work. So the shopaholic hits the mall almost daily to avoid discussing uncomfortable issues with her partner, the internet addict spends another afternoon alone in his room in order to avoid the anxiety of meeting new people, and the pothead avoids the stress of thinking about her legal troubles by getting high all day. Temporarily these things work. And then they don't. The high goes away, but the problems remain. So to avoid the problem that won't go away, the compulsive behaver shops, surfs, or smokes more and more. All the while old problems persist, and new problems begin and grow. But the highs that once lasted days now last hours, and those that lasted hours last minutes. Over time the highs are greatly reduced, and the problems you've been avoiding become compounded. And so the cycle continues. Temporary highs do not solve problems. Problem solving does.

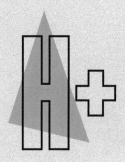

TIP N°2

GET HIGH ON HEALTHY

You can get the same euphoric feeling drugs produce from healthy activities like running, boxing, or lifting weights. Like drugs, these activities release the mood-altering substances known as endorphins into the body, stimulating the pleasure centers of the brain and creating a healthy and productive "high" you can enjoy safely. So go ahead. Everyone's doing it.

---

3. Compulsive Behaviors Persist Despite Negative Consequences

Angie was aware that she was more than 100 pounds overweight, but she continued to eat compulsively anyway. Smokers know how dangerous cigarettes are, but still they smoke. And gamblers know the pain of losing it all, but the next day they head back to the track to blow it all again. But why? Why do people engage in these behaviors despite the negative consequences? Contrary to what you might think, it's not because they're weak or without willpower. Compulsive shoppers know shopping several hours per day, several days per week is not good for them, and sometimes they try to reduce or stop the behavior. But, despite their intense effort, they often fail. That's because they've developed a dependence on the behavior that only grows worse over time.

4. Compulsive Behaviors Take on a Life of their Own

Functional autonomy is a term used to describe how some behaviors begin for one reason but then continue to function on their own (autonomy) long after the reason they began ceases to be an issue. Let's say Naomi starts vaping at 14 due to peer pressure from her friends. If she is still vaping at 44, three decades after the peer pressure from her friends has stopped, then her compulsive behavior has taken on a life of its own. She has become physically addicted to the chemicals and psychologically addicted to the brief buzz smoking gives her. She also believes that her smoking reduces her stress, which it does for just a few minutes. Worse, even though she no longer needs to smoke to fit in, she sees herself as a smoker. If she were to create a list of adjectives that describe who she is, *smoker* would make the list. Some people *are* gamblers, and some *are* drinkers. If you reach a point when the compulsive behaviors begin to merge with your identity, they can be hard to give up.

Do you have any compulsive behaviors that you hope you won't still be engaging in when you are older? If you want to prevent long-term problems in the future, your best bet is to get a hold of them now and stop them before they grow out of control.

5. Compulsive Behaviors Follow a Predictable Pattern

If you want to break the hold your compulsions have on you, you'll need to recognize their pattern, a four-stage cycle that repeats until the pattern of behavior is broken.

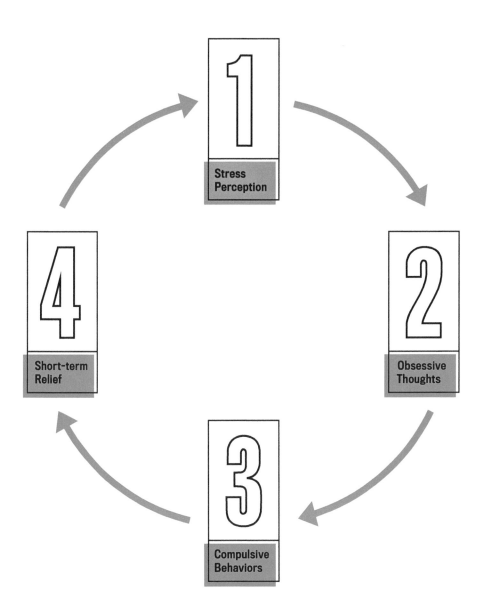

If you identify where your behaviors fall on the cycle, you can identify how they evolved and how you can intervene to get them under control. To practice, let's see how Angie's compulsive eating fits into these four stages.

STAGE 1
STRESS PERCEPTION

Here, Angie perceives some external event in her life—her husband's inattentiveness to her or her son's temper tantrums— as unacceptable, unmanageable, or emotionally undesirable.

others, food provides a reward, an escape from life's ills. As long as the unhealthy choice is rewarded by temporary relief— a food high, in her case—Angie will remain unmotivated to develop more lasting long-term solutions to her problems.

STAGE 2
OBSESSIVE THOUGHTS

Angie begins to have internal dialogue in which she belittles herself over her unattractiveness as a lover or her ineffectiveness as a parent. This dialogue presents her with two options: either tackle her issues head on by speaking to her husband about her concerns and finding more effective ways to discipline her son; or avoid her discomfort by overeating.

STAGE 3
COMPULSIVE BEHAVIORS

Angie can anticipate short-term relief from her pain and stress by overeating. For her and many

STAGE 4
SHORT-TERM RELIEF

As Angie enters this stage, she experiences some relief from her overeating, and life seems better—for the moment. After the high from overeating has passed and the reality of what she has just done sets in, feelings of guilt begin. Angie has told herself hundreds of times that this was the last time, and here she is again sick from cheeseburgers and milkshakes and covered with empty chocolate wrappers. And the problems she wanted to avoid are still there. She has sought short-term relief instead of long-term solutions. Without a change in this pattern, Angie's cycle will repeat again and again.

Breaking the Cycle: Three Ways to Move from Compulsion to Real Emotional Change

Take a minute to think about yourself. Do you have a behavior you turn to compulsively when you need to escape your emotions? Do you vape, drink, use drugs, cut yourself, shoplift, shop, practice unsafe sex, gamble, or play video games compulsively? Does this behavior prevent you from doing things you want and need to do? Could this behavior lead to worse effects than it already has? Like an anesthetic, these behaviors numb the pain for a limited time, but then they wear off quickly, and a tolerance builds up. Angie was more than 100 pounds overweight before she realized she needed to seek help. But you don't have to get to this stage. If you answered "yes" to any of the previous questions, consider changing your feelings safely by one or more of these three healthy alternatives to engaging in dangerous compulsive behaviors.

1. Process Your Emotions Naturally

One way to relieve some of your emotional discomfort is to engage your sensory motor system, in other words, to process your emotions in a way that feels natural and good for your body. You can laugh, cry, scream, run, or relax to create an emotional change. Your friend passed away? Cry your eyes out. You just lost the championship? Go for a long walk and be alone for a while. When Angie vowed to get better, she allowed herself to cry when she was hurt and to laugh when she felt good. She started walking every day to lose weight, and she's just begun practicing yoga. She's more relaxed than she has been in years.

For many people, talking to a trusted loved one or friend is a healthy, natural way to process emotions. Some people talk to their spouses or partners. Others talk to their parents or siblings. Sometimes when you're feeling down and

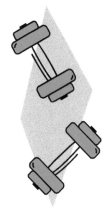

out, having a good friend to help you make sense of your feelings is just what the doctor ordered. Come to think of it, some people even talk to doctors, like me as a matter of fact! Whoever it is, find someone you trust, and tell them what's on your mind.

Of course, one of the most fun ways to process your emotions in a healthy way is exercise. Basketball, jogging, or competitive line dancing: It doesn't matter what you do, just as long as you move! The brain's release of endorphins will feel great, and you'll want to do it again and again. Just be careful, though. Engaging in aggressive behaviors—like punching walls, for instance—is a counterproductive and dangerous way to release your aggression. Try channeling that anger into something productive and safe, like boxing or weightlifting. Also, be aware that exercise and other positive behaviors are just as problematic when they are treated compulsively. You can be as addicted to diet and exercise as you can be to overeating and lying around, so practice all good things in moderation.

2. Change the Way You Think

Let's look at two different ways you can use your thoughts to change the way you feel. First, you can adjust your mindset, which means you should simply move your thoughts away from your obsessive thinking onto something else. Even a short change in mindset can provide temporary relief, but a long-term adjustment can have wonderful, lasting impacts on how you feel. Where your focus goes, your energy and feelings are sure to follow. Take a "time out" after a heated argument. Read a magazine article to get your mind off your dad's layoff at work. Volunteer at the cancer ward after your uncle is diagnosed with it. These activities will help break the cycle of compulsive behaviors and negative self-talk and will impact your emotional state for the better.

Second, although changing your mindset works in the short term, the long-term method involves changing your emotional obsessions and moving away from unhealthy thinking patterns. Angie's way of thinking went something like this: *I am worthless and disgusting. I deserve to be abused and taken advantage of. My husband doesn't love me, and my son doesn't respect me. I am just fat and undesirable. Why take care of myself anyway? To be attractive only means that men will hurt me again, just like my uncle did.* This way of thinking and its resultant overeating imprisons Angie, and if she's not careful, it could kill her. Angie will not be able to break away from her compulsive behavior until she breaks free from her thought patterns. While a mindset shift may relieve her emotional pain temporarily, the odds are that Angie will relapse into her old ways if she does not make more permanent changes.

Angie must practice positive thinking and truly believing these new thoughts. She must tell herself: *I have value. Even if I am overweight, I deserve to be loved. No one has the right to take advantage of me. I will improve my relationships with my husband and my son, and I will take care of my mind and body for my own sake. I must love myself so others can love me, too.* It may be difficult or feel unnatural at first, but you, too, can practice positive thinking. But allowing yourself to continue down a path of self-destruction through negative self-talk is not an option. Every time you catch yourself starting to talk negatively to yourself or others, you must make a concerted effort to substitute positive self-talk in its place. You'll like how it feels.

3. You Can Take Drugs

Wait, wait! I know what you're thinking: *But Dr. Cortman, haven't you been telling me this whole time* not *to take drugs?* I just wanted to make sure I still have your attention. The drugs I'm referring to here are not what you were thinking. Instead of heroin, cocaine, or methamphetamine, some people struggling with mental health or other emotional issues take medications prescribed by doctors. For patients struggling with severe anxiety, clinical depression, addiction, or personality disorders, it is sometimes necessary to carefully prescribe mood-altering controlled substances. These drugs are often clinically necessary and quite helpful, but they are to be used with extreme caution and under the strict supervision of a doctor. Even for those who require chemical assistance, healthy, natural approaches to processing emotions and thoughts are still in order. Were Angie to self medicate and only use diet pills to solve her weight problem while ignoring her underlying thoughts and behaviors, she would not have targeted the root cause of her issues and would continue her destructive cycle. To compound her problems, she might also develop another problem in the process: a pill addiction. The bottom line: Drugs of these kinds should be viewed as a last resort, not a first one; they should be used as an *aid* to wellness, not as a cure-all; and they should be used only under the care of a doctor.

Diving Deep
Beneath the Surface

Whether you choose to address your behaviors on your own—by engaging in positive alternative behaviors and practicing positive self-talk, for example—or you seek the help of a professional, you are going to have to address your underlying emotional issues at some point before they spiral out of control. And let's be clear: Addressing things can be difficult and painful work. You will bring some buried emotional issues to the surface, and you must confront them. Angie had to reckon with her childhood abandonment and subsequent abuse. These traumas retained their hold on her into her adulthood and affected her relationships and almost all other aspects of her life. She developed bad behaviors and a negative self-image, and she would probably have eaten herself to death over time if she had not admitted she had a problem and sought help.

Angie wrestled with her emotions in therapy, stopped herself in negative self-talk and replaced it with positive, and took up exercise and other hobbies to replace compulsive eating. She takes a mild antidepressant under supervision, and she meditates, does yoga, and practices deep breathing to reduce stress. She still sees her therapist on occasion, but she has learned through therapy how to release some of her anger and pain on her own. Her relationships with her husband and son have improved, and she is well on her way to physical fitness and psychological recovery. Her journey is not over, however. Angie will have to keep in mind these principles forever. She must never allow herself to slide back into her old habits, her old ways of being. Getting healthy is difficult enough. Staying healthy is even harder. But Angie is doing it, and you can, too.

Now let's focus on some exercises that will help you change your thoughts and feelings and stop your compulsive behaviors.

———

EXERCISES

In this chapter you learned about the connections between thoughts, feelings, beliefs, and behaviors. You learned that emotions impact your life in different ways. They can move you forward in a healthy and productive direction, or they can overwhelm you and cause you to make unwise choices. Let's do some work to set you in the right direction.

1 How do You Cope?

This first exercise is simple. Simply identify the behaviors, good or bad, that you turn to when times are hard and you want to feel better. Do you cry, sleep, throw things, eat junk food, play video games? Do you jog, meditate, lift weights, dance? List as many as you can.

1. _____

2. _____

3. _____

4. _____

5. _____

6. _____

7. _____

8. _____

9. _____

10. _____

11. _____

12. _____

13. _____

14. _____

15. _____

② Be Real with Yourself

The first step to improve yourself is admitting something needs to be improved. Here you should try to be as honest with yourself as possible. Below, identify one of each of the potential problem behaviors.

Compulsive Behavior

From your previous list, select a behavior you engage in when you are feeling emotionally unwell that you know does not solve your problems and often makes them worse (drugs, alcohol, or nicotine use; unsafe sex; gambling; shoplifting; cutting; etc). Describe it in a sentence or two.

_____

_____

_____

_____

_____

Unhealthy Habit

Next, describe an unhealthy habit you have that you would like to change (bad hygiene, diet, or sleep habits; exercise avoidance; excessive internet or social media usage; etc.)

_____

_____

_____

_____

_____

Other Area to Work On

Describe any other area of your life you would like to improve (relationships with parents, attendance and performance at school, performance on the field, etc.).

_____

_____

_____

_____

_____

3 The Cycle that Goes Nowhere

Let's map out the compulsive behavior you identified above (or another one, if you wish) in terms of the four stages of progression from stress perception to short-term relief.

Stress Perception

List the things and people that cause you to feel stressed, hurt, or emotionally unwell.

1. _____

2. _____

3. _____

4. _____

5. _____

Obsessive Thoughts

Select one of the above stressors and describe the kinds of thoughts you think when you feel this stress. If it helps, write your thoughts like a monologue to yourself.

_____

_____

_____

_____

Compulsive Behaviors

Describe the behaviors you engage in when you want to avoid your perceived stress and your obsessive thoughts.

_____

_____

_____

_____

Short-term Relief

Describe how you feel when you engage in this behavior. Do you feel a sort of high? Do you feel like your problems are resolved? Or do you struggle with feelings of guilt and regret from engaging in the behavior and from additional problems the behavior may have created? Be specific.

_____

_____

_____

_____

4 Making the Change

Positive Self-talk

Instead of getting stuck in your obsessive thoughts, what are some things you could say to yourself that would help you get out of that rut? Use this opportunity to create a new script for yourself.

_____

_____

_____

Healthy Behaviors

What are some healthy behaviors and activities you can engage in next time you feel yourself going to that dark place? What positive behaviors can replace your compulsive ones? Try to list 10, and feel free to include ones you already engage in.

1. _____

2. _____

3. _____

4. _____

5. _____

6. _____

7. _____

8. _____

9. _____

10. _____

Plan Your Work and Work Your Plan

Using positive self-talk and your list of alternative behaviors, describe your plan of action for the next time you begin to feel stressed or emotionally unwell. What will you do to ensure you do not get caught in the cycle of repeating ineffective and destructive behaviors next time you're feeling down? Come up with a plan. Be specific.

_____

_____

_____

_____

_____

_____

_____

_____

_____

_____

_____

_____

_____

_____

_____

Getting at the Roots

Now that you have a plan of action, think hard one more time about the root cause of your pain and emotional problems. Is it that you are being abused in a bad relationship? Are you grieving the recent death of a good friend? Your symptoms of pain and suffering will not go away until you address their root cause head on. So how will you do that? Take a few minutes to describe exactly what you need to change in your life and how you will do it so you can be happy and well.

_____

_____

_____

_____

_____

_____

_____

_____

_____

_____

_____

_____

_____

_____

TRUTH N° 3

Every Behavior Has a Purpose (and It's Not Always What You Think)

Recently Kyla began to develop a bad relationship with shopping. When she was 13, Kyla's parents often dropped her and her friends off at the mall, usually giving Kyla $50 to spend on whatever she wanted. She always spent nearly every dime they gave her on makeup, clothes, accessories for her phone, lunch, and the like. Sometimes she spent more than $50 and had to borrow a few dollars from her friends, who sometimes gave her a hard time for it. Tragically, when Kyla was 15, her father became ill and passed away. When she was 16, Kyla began working part time at the little smoothie place near her house to help her mom with the bills and to save a little money. Kyla still works there, bringing home around $300 every two weeks. She gives $100 to her mom for bills and spends the other $200 at the mall, usually on payday, every single time. She's been working there almost two years and has nothing saved. She owes her friends $140 for things they bought her recently, and a few times the $100 she promised her mom was more like $70 or $80.

A few months ago, Kyla started shoplifting. It started with a cell phone charger and a dare from her friends. Minutes later, she stole lip gloss and a change purse from one store, and then a pair of jeans from a display outside another one. Within twenty minutes Kyla had stolen more merchandise than she could have bought with her own money. On her next payday, Kyla entered the mall around noon with a backpack and $198.75. After two hours she walked out with 12 pairs of earrings, four phone cases, two pairs of high-end sunglasses, a gold bracelet, two designer shirts, and a new pair of running shoes. And $198.75. The next day she went to the mall across town and did the same thing. Whole outfits, lacy underwear, an expensive designer purse. It was a huge rush. It was also very dangerous. Kyla almost got caught twice before she left quickly to avoid security.

Kyla is a smart girl. She knows her actions are illegal and could land her in jail, but she continues to steal almost every day. Why? What could possibly possess this otherwise kind, generous, and hardworking girl to commit actual misdemeanors and felonies on a regular basis? This is extreme behavior, no doubt, but it has a purpose. All behavior does. If Kyla wants to avoid serious consequences, she must identify and confront what motivates her to steal so habitually so she can move forward with her life in an honest and productive manner.

We'll examine the reasons behind Kyla's risky behavior in the next section. First, consider the following questions, and see if you can imagine what would motivate someone to act in the following ways.

Why would Natalie steal a blade from her dad's work bench, cut the skin on her bicep a dozen times, and watch herself bleed until she almost passes out? Why would Anthony spend an entire weekend scrolling through Netflix, watching mostly the previews and maybe a couple shows, but doing nothing otherwise? Why would Diane nag her children when she knows it provokes them and pushes them away? And why would Danny wear the same smelly, unwashed T-shirt under his baseball uniform for an entire season?

The answer in each case is simple: For each person, the behavior—no matter how strange or illogical it may seem—meets a need. For instance, Natalie may cut herself because focusing on physical pain provides her short relief from the emotional pain she experiences from having been abused as a child. Because she has had so much pain inflicted on her by others, Natalie has chosen to take back some of the power she has lost by inflicting the pain on herself instead of allowing others to do it. The cutting causes an emotional purge, which gives her a sense of release from inner pain. Because the cutting meets this need, Natalie will likely continue to practice this behavior.

Other motivations are easier to understand. Maybe Anthony just doesn't want to do the homework he's been behind on for two weeks. His mom said he can't leave the house until it's finished, so he stays in his room avoiding his task and wasting his time. Diane hounds her children because when she was a child, her mother often left her home alone in their apartment for entire weekends, and she remembers the terror of having no one to meet her needs or to comfort her while she wept loudly for hours. She vowed long ago never to neglect her children, but she must be careful she does not push them away in the process. And Danny is superstitious, plain and simple. He pitched the only no-hitter of his career while wearing one of the undershirts his girlfriend gave him for his birthday the week before. Though he's not completely sure, he feels pretty confident the shirt gave him good luck. He had a great game that day—and he's played well ever since—so he doesn't want to risk it. Until he has reason to suspect otherwise, he's content continuing to believe that a stinky T-shirt is the reason for his success.

All behavior makes sense to us on some level at the time we engage in it. But even if you don't fully understand *why* you do what you do, at least understand that the behavior is meeting some particular need or you would not do it. The key is figuring out what this need is and addressing it.

Purposeful *Mis*behavior

Consider the purpose of lying. We lie when we are afraid of the consequences of telling the truth. My colleague Dr. Jill Scarpellini shares an example of the purposefulness of lying that occurred around the time this behavior usually first appears. After stepping out of the room to take a phone call, Jill walked back into the room where her 2-year-old son had been playing alone for a few minutes. Books and toys were everywhere. Jill was a bit startled by the transformation that had taken place in her formerly neat room. Her son saw his mother observing the room and said to her, "Mess!" Jill asked her son, "How do you think it got this way?" Her son, afraid of the consequences of telling the truth, responded, "Daddy!"

Think about why people gossip. Passing on rumors about people raises your status in a group by making it seem as if you have interesting information about others who are not present. Dr. Marion Underwood, author of *Social Aggression Among Girls* [2] explains that gossiping and spreading rumors about others is "an effective way to be aggressive without facing social sanctions." In other words, people talk trash and get away with it, so they do it again.

Students cheat on tests to avoid the consequences of not studying. People cheat on partners because they feel unwanted or unimportant in their relationships. And children throw fits to gain someone's attention. Even if the reasons are not clear, no behavior is random. Remember: Every behavior has an underlying purpose, but it's not always what you think.

So what about Kyla? What could she possibly stand to gain from taking such drastic risks to her freedom? Sure, the outfits and the jewelry are nice—and there is such a rush to the whole thing—but something deeper must be going on. Kyla is not a bad kid at all. She's a great student, and she helps her mom around the house almost every day. She volunteers at a pet shelter and tutors freshmen in math once a week. So what gives? Why this illegal—and dangerous—behavior? Well, the answer is a bit compli-cated. Kyla grew up somewhat poor. She always had the necessities, but her parents never really had much more. The money they gave her to go to the mall was the most they could offer, but she was their only daughter, and they wanted her to enjoy some small pleasures in life. Kyla's friends' parents were always much better off than Kyla's parents, so her friends always had money to spend. They bought nice things—lots of nice things—and Kyla just couldn't keep up. This made her feel insecure and ashamed. Her friends gave her a hard time about borrow-ing money beyond what her parents had given her. The teasing embarrassed her. This cycle of insecurity, shame, and embarrassment lasted several years, until her father died when she was 15.

Of course, Kyla was crushed. Her dad was her rock, the one who protected her and kept her on the right track. The one who spoiled her and loved her and helped her be her best. And then he was gone. So was his guidance and support and messages of love and approval. And so was his money. So, poorer than ever and without her moral role model to show her the way, Kyla began to steal. And for the first time ever, she didn't have to watch her spending, she didn't have to borrow from her friends, and she didn't have to get the off-brand jacket when she really wanted the designer one. Kyla can save her money and still have everything she wants. She fits in with her friends, and she stands out at school. Her new clothes and jewelry mean new attention from the boys she wants to date and the girls she wants to be friends with. Kyla's mother is grieving and working twice as many hours as before to support her daughter, so she has lost track where Kyla is and who she's with most of the time. Most of all, the attention Kyla gets at school and on social media and the hanging out she does on the weekends all keep her from properly mourning the loss of her beloved father. If she's texting her friends or trying on her new clothes, then she's not crying hysterically. But Kyla has already had several close calls with security guards, and her mother has recently become suspicious of her new wardrobe and accessories. If she does not address her grief and the role it plays in causing her risky behavior, Kyla may find herself wearing an unflattering shade of orange in the near future.

Avoidance Feels Good Now (But Terrible Later)

We all avoid things from time to time: the dishes, homework, apologizing. Avoidance is a common behavior that provides short-term relief. The inconvenience you might incur now by taking your dog for a walk can be put off until later if you take a nap or watch a movie instead. Of course, the problem will still be there when you wake up.

Much like a drug provides temporary reprieve from uncomfortable feelings or situations, avoidance techniques can help you put off until later what you're running from now, but eventually your issues will catch up with you and you won't be able to avoid them any longer. Escapist techniques will not solve problems, so the cycle will continue.

Unless you really examine your behavior closely and deeply, you may not realize your purpose is avoidance. Kyla could have found a dozen reasons to justify her shoplifting—the outfits, the excitement, the money she was saving—but unless she takes a close, honest look at herself, she may not realize that her behavior is mostly an attempt to avoid her grief—she wouldn't be stealing with her dad around. Her actions may work in the short term, but Kyla will have to accept her father's death and grieve in a healthy, if painful, manner. To do otherwise could have major implications in Kyla's life. Unfortunately, we don't often think about the motivations for our actions in these ways, so we continue the cycle of counterproductive behaviors. The sooner you confront what you've been avoiding, the sooner you reduce the chance of having to deal with it again.

An Unwillingness to Move On

We all have things we want to hold on to—an ex-boyfriend's sweater, a cheap necklace a friend gave you before she moved away, that old blanket from early childhood—and hanging on to a cherished item in most cases is harmless enough. Refusing to let go of negative emotions, on the other hand, can have serious consequences for your mental health. For example, anger may seem like an emotion everyone would want to move on from, but many people hold on to it much longer than is healthy or necessary.

Take De'Andre, for example. Two years ago, De'Andre had an altercation with his brother Eric that turned violent. De'Andre borrowed $50 and promised to repay it, but never did. Eric asked for it back, words were exchanged, and De'Andre pushed his brother to the ground. In the two years since they last spoke, De'Andre has remained angry at Eric, even after Eric has tried to reach out to him several times. By holding on to his anger, De'Andre can continue to avoid apologizing for, or even acknowledging, the role he played in the fight, and by refusing to apologize, he can continue to believe that he is the victim. De'Andre believes that releasing his anger with his brother will be an admission that Eric was right, and he was wrong. Because of his unwillingness to let this go, De'Andre feels angry almost all the time. What's worse, he's chosen to remain angry over having a relationship with his brother.

Self-protection is another reason people sometimes don't let go of emotions. Jackie believes that when she lets people into her life, she is making herself vulnerable to mistreatment. Jackie is 19, finishing her sophomore year in college. She had two boyfriends in high school—one during freshman year, the other when she was a sophomore. Unfortunately, both boys cheated on Jackie, and she was badly hurt and felt publicly humiliated both times. The trauma she endured caused Jackie to swear off dating and meeting young guys, so she hasn't had a meaningful relationship with any male in more than four years. Jackie would like to release her anger and move on with her life, but to do so would be to take a risk she's not sure she can handle. Instead, Jackie stays aloof and closed off to avoid the possibility of future pain.

People hold on to emotions for many reasons. Mr. Jeffries clings to humiliations he suffered in school as a child. After vowing never to be humiliated again, he instead maintains strict control over the students he now teaches, never allowing a student to step out of line. Unfortunately, each day is a struggle for Mr. Jeffries, as he suppresses his pain by expending exhausting amounts of energy to maintain discipline and order. Pedro holds on to the pain of losing his brother over a decade ago because he believes that to end his mourning would be a dishonor to his brother. As a mistaken tribute, Pedro is gloomy almost every day and has few friends. And Stacy hangs on to the fearful memories of a time when she was very young and an airplane she was on experienced engine failure and rough turbulence. Even though she is now an adult who knows all kinds of information about the safety of air travel, she clings to her old fears to avoid facing new ones. Not surprisingly, Stacy hasn't been many places, and all her best friends are doing exciting things without her.

Sometimes people hang on to emotions because that's what they have been taught to do. Take the emotion of guilt, for example. Most people don't like to feel bad about what they have done, so they straighten up their act and let go of the guilt. But some people are raised to believe that they are responsible for how others feel and behave, and when things don't go well, they feel guilty. If, "Mommy and Daddy are upset because you were a bad little girl" and "How could you *do* such a thing?" were the kinds of refrains you heard as a child, then you may end up living your life believing everything is your fault. You may hang on to misplaced guilt simply because you don't know how to let it go and because you believe that without it you would allow yourself to do bad things. It is important to realize, however, that: Most things are not your fault; how people feel and behave is up to them; and you probably already know how to behave properly without needlessly wracking yourself with unnecessary guilt. Take my advice: Just let the guilt go.

Don't Worry, We Didn't Forget Worry

What purpose does worrying serve, and why would anyone want to suffer from anxiety or insomnia because they can't stop doing it? While everyone worries about something every now and then, many people are chronic worriers. Most people will tell you that they hate to worry all the time, but they just can't help it. While it is possible to control your worrying, you must also understand that it serves a very clear purpose. Worry tells you that you perceive that some threat may bring harm to you or someone you care about. Sometimes these threats are beyond your control, and sometimes they are not. In either case, worrying needlessly will not help.

For example, let's say Denise sends her daughter Jennifer back to college after winter break. While Jennifer is at 30,000 feet, Denise is pacing her living room with a drink in her hand. She cannot rest easy until Jennifer lands and calls her to say she's safe. What should be obvious is that Denise's pacing and drinking will have no influence over whether the plane crashes or lands safely. While Denise's worry is a sign that someone she cares about may be at risk, she must recognize she can do nothing about the situation. To ease her mind, Denise would be much wiser to engage in a fun and healthy activity like watching a movie or walking to the museum with a friend for a few hours until she hears from Jennifer.

Now let's look at Ronnie's situation. Ronnie is a freshman in college, and right now his grades are not looking so hot. Currently, Ronnie has a D in English and an F in chemistry. He has a 10-page paper on a novel he didn't read due on Monday, and his chemistry lab final is on Tuesday. Ronnie has spent most of this semester at the gym with his friends or at the movies with his girlfriend. He's done almost none of his assignments or prior labs and has not prepared in any way for what he must do over the next few days. As you might expect, Ronnie is very worried. It's Saturday afternoon, and Ronnie spent most of last night and all of this morning worried and unable to focus on his studies. Since he's been messing around all semester, everything he's reading seems new to him. He has no idea how to even begin the English paper, and simply not blowing himself up in the lab next week will be a major accomplishment. Ronnie has several options available—he has friends who can help him study, there are tutors in the library and learning centers on campus—(Heck, you can even rent the movie, Ronnie!)—but he is stuck in the frenzied state of worry and confusion, and he's getting absolutely nothing done.

In Ronnie's case, just as in Denise's, worry lets him know something is at risk. Unlike Denise, however, Ronnie can do something about it. Instead of allowing the worrying to prevent his progress in this time of crisis, Ronnie should channel his energy into making the absolute best of his bad situation. He should realize that much is at stake, so he will have to act decisively if he wants to save his grades. If Ronnie is smart, he will learn from this experience and change his habits immediately.

Many people struggle with understanding their emotions, and worry is no different. While Denise could tell you she's worried about Jennifer, and Ronnie could tell you he's worried about getting kicked out of school before he's even had a chance to prove himself, neither seems to realize that their worry is just a sign that something is at risk. More to the point, if the plane lands safely, or if Ronnie somehow passes his test, Denise and Ronnie may mistakenly believe that their worry was what brought about success, and they may be inclined to do it again the next time something comes up. In psychology, when someone believes that two things that occur together are associated, even if they are unrelated, we call this the Law of Association. Let's say it's raining outside while I'm eating my lunch, and I choke on my sandwich and almost pass out. If I begin to believe that the rain caused me to choke and vow never to eat during a rainstorm again, this would be a mistaken belief in the Law of Association. A funny example of this belief comes from the classic children's television show *Sesame Street*. In one episode, Bert tries to talk to Ernie, who can't hear him because he has a banana in his ear. When asked why he has a banana in his ear, Ernie responds, "I use this banana to keep the alligators away." Bert responds, "Alligators?!? Ernie, there

are no alligators on Sesame Street." Ernie's response? "Right. It's doing a good job, isn't it, Bert?" It's best to avoid this kind of superstitious thinking.

On the other hand, if Denise realizes she can do nothing to change her daughter's situation and that worrying will only make her feel worse, she can focus her time and energy on something positive instead. If Ronnie realizes that his worry and continued procrastination only make the problem worse by the minute and that he *can* do something about it, he may instead decide to set his mind to accomplishing a couple very difficult tasks in a short period of time and pledge to never allow himself to misplace his priorities again. If both Denise and Ronnie follow this advice, worry will have served its purpose in a positive way.

———

[2]   Underwood, Marion K. *Social Aggression Among Girls*. New York: The Guilford Press, 2003.

FIND YOUR PURPOSE

Many people believe if they can figure out why they are here, then life will be more fulfilling and meaningful. And while each person's purpose is theirs to decide, the truth is that discovering one's purpose is a journey, sometimes a lifelong one, that takes a great deal of focus and effort to navigate successfully. Although finding your purpose is a noble goal, it is important to note that the goal of this book is to help you focus on the small steps that can help make finding your purpose, or purposes, a little easier. If you can figure out why you use drugs, skip class, engage in unsafe sex, punch walls, or stay up nights worrying about things beyond your control, then you can address the real causes of your problems. When you remove these painful obstacles from your life, you will free yourself to begin spending your time in ways that are meaningful and fulfilling to you. The following exercises may help you do this.

EXERCISES

———

For these exercises to work, you must be honest with yourself. This self-reflection may be difficult, but it is a necessary part of the process of becoming who you want to be. We suggest you take this survey now and then again in the future after you've had some time to work on some of the strategies outlined in this chapter. Count your **Yes** responses now and see if the number is lower over time. If it is, keep going; you are on the right track!

① Scratching the Surface

Anger

Do you find yourself becoming angry
or furious at least once per day?   YES   NO

Do you find yourself feeling good,
relieved, or satisfied after being angry?   YES   NO

Do you become angry frequently
but rarely ask yourself why?   YES   NO

Do people often have to tell you to
calm down or that you have a bad temper?   YES   NO

Fear & Anxiety

Do you find yourself feeling anxious
or afraid at least once per day?   YES   NO

Do you find yourself thinking about your
fears and anxieties even when you aren't afraid?   YES   NO

Do you ever tell yourself you have a right
to be afraid without examining why you are?   YES   NO

Do your fears and anxieties sometimes
prevent you from doing things you want to do?   YES   NO

Worry

Is it fair to describe you as a chronic
worrier? Do people say you worry too much?   YES   NO

When you worry, is there a sense
that bad things are going to happen?   YES   NO

Do you sometimes think,
Of course I worry, the world is a scary place?   YES   NO

Does your worrying sometimes prevent
you from doing things you want to do?   YES   NO

Self-pity

Do you often feel sorry for yourself?
Do you often feel you have been victimized?   YES   NO

Does talking about those who take
advantage of you feel good, like a form of payback?   YES   NO

Do you often feel like it's not your fault other people
are terrible and that there's nothing you can do?   YES   NO

Does your self-pity turn others off?
Do they avoid you or tell you to "get over" stuff?   YES   NO

Count how many **Yes** answers you have. Implement the advice in this chapter to
try to lower the number of **Yes** responses over time.

    /   16
_____

2 Digging In

To make use of this chapter's Social Black Belt Truth,
you need to figure out your behaviors' true purposes.
Here you will discover why you engage in behavior
that has negative consequences.

List three behaviors you repeatedly engage in when dealing with people or
situations that cause you stress.

1. _____

2. _____

3. _____

When you are feeling especially emotional—angry, sad, or anxious, for example—
what negative behaviors help you release your pent-up emotions?

1. _____

2. _____

3. _____

What behaviors do you exhibit that others have told you are unhealthy or that
you should stop?

1. _____

2. _____

3. _____

3 Going Deeper

Select one of the above behaviors that you most want to stop. Answer the following questions in a few sentences or a short paragraph if possible.

Behavior: _____

Why do you engage in this behavior? What purpose does it serve? What are you avoiding or hoping to accomplish when you behave this way?

_____

_____

_____

_____

_____

_____

Where did you learn this behavior? What in your life allows for this behavior to continue?

_____

_____

_____

_____

_____

_____

What skills do you need to develop to help you stop this negative behavior (i.e., assertiveness, patience, independence, trust in others, etc.)? What behaviors could you engage in that would be positive and healthy replacements for the negative behavior you currently engage in?

_____

_____

_____

_____

_____

_____

TRUTH N° 4

Sometimes Your Worst Enemy is *You*

Tevin and Derek sat together at lunch on Monday. "Man, Tev, Mrs. Jones' math test was crazy. I studied all week and I *still* had a hard time with it."

"I'm sure you did alright, D. What's for lunch?"

"Ham and cheese, pretzel rods, applesauce, juice. And a note from my mom that shall forever remain a secret. What about you?"

"Fruit cup, YumCakes, chips, and peanut butter and jelly. Man, I *hate* peanut butter and jelly."

On Tuesday it was the same thing. Derek had ham and cheese, and Tevin complained about peanut butter and jelly. Wednesday the same, and Thursday as well. Finally, on Friday, after it looked like Tevin was about to blow his stack over yet another peanut butter and jelly sandwich, Derek asked nervously, "Hey bro, I know this is none of my business, but if you hate PB&J that much, why don't you just ask your mom to pack you something else?"

"Leave my mom out of this, Derek," Tevin responded angrily. "I pack my own lunch."

No doubt you've known someone like Tevin who acts in ways that are clearly not in his or her best interest. You may have a friend who confounds you and others because she constantly seems to do things that appear calculated to get her in trouble, often the same kind of trouble time and again. Maybe this behavior even describes you. If you're like most people, you've probably done things that seem counterintuitive or irrational, even while the logical part of your brains screams, *Wait, don't do it!* So, what's going on here? What would cause you or anyone else to sabotage a good situation or to act in ways that you know to be destructive? Let's consider Josh's story to see if we can gain some insight into this strange behavior.

Josh was 19 and in his freshman year of college when he was partnered in the chemistry lab with the girl from class he'd been checking out since the first day of the semester. Jasmine was smart, beautiful, and passionate about science, just like Josh. In other words, she was everything he was looking for in a girlfriend. After working with Jasmine for several weeks in the lab, Josh finally gathered the courage to ask her on a date. Much to Josh's surprise, Jasmine said yes. They exchanged numbers after class, and, after texting each other for a couple days, finally decided to meet up with their mutual friends Erica and Steve for a double date to watch their school's basketball team take on their chief rival for the conference championship and to go together to a huge celebration party afterward if their team won.

The game was close and very exciting. Jasmine was so nervous that she clung tightly to Josh the whole game, squeezing his hand and looking to him for assurance that their team would come through in the end. With a last second desperation shot, Josh and Jasmine's school won by two points, and the crowd went crazy. Jasmine jumped up and screamed with excitement. She gave Josh a huge hug and a kiss on the cheek before joining the raucous celebration on the floor. Josh stood in amazement, vowing to himself never to wash his face again. He was smitten.

The afterparty was even better. Josh and Jasmine danced together the whole time, only taking breaks to walk outside together when one of them needed a rest and some fresh air. It was almost dawn when Josh walked Jasmine back to her dorm—holding hands the whole time. They sat on her steps for an hour, talking about everything under the sun. Josh realized it was getting late—or early—when the girls in Jasmine's dorm started waking up and heading out to their 8 a.m. classes. Realizing his date with Jasmine was officially coming to an end, Josh did what just days ago would have seemed an impossible fantasy: He leaned in and kissed the girl he'd been crushing on for months. *I am officially in love,* he thought.

If at this point you're assuming Josh and Jasmine dated for a while and then broke up; or dated for a while, got married, and lived happily ever after; or even dated for a while before Jasmine cheated on Josh with the 6' 4" point guard who hit the game-winning shot, you would be wrong, wrong, and wrong again. So what exactly did happen, then, after Josh and Jasmine's magical first date? Well, quite simply, Josh ignored Jasmine's calls and texts, the semester ended, and Jasmine, heartbroken and confused by Josh's total 180, transferred schools—partly to be closer to home and partly to be farther away from the painful reminders of being ignored by the dorky science guy who took her out for the most perfect night of her life.

So what gives? Why in the world would Josh pine over a girl for months, finally work up the courage to ask her out, share a magical evening with her, and then disappear without a trace? His inner saboteur made him do it, of course. You see, somewhere inside of Josh, like somewhere inside all of us, is a little voice that constantly reminds him about all the things that could possibly go wrong, even in a good situation. When things are going well for Josh, as they were with Jasmine, his saboteur says, *Don't do it, Josh. Don't answer her texts, and don't ask her out again. What if she realizes she doesn't like you that much? She'll reject you, and you'll be hurt and embarrassed. Even worse, what if she says yes? You'll have a great time with her, you'll fall in love, and you'll probably have a great relationship. But then what? Eventually she'll realize that you're not that cute, not that funny, and not that smart. She'll find someone else, and she'll leave you. And what will you have then? A broken heart, that's what. The best thing you can do is to just end it before it starts. No need to put yourself through all that pain, Josh. Just walk away.*

Unfortunately, what happened to Josh happens to many of us. We have a good thing going, and then we do everything in our power to tear it down. We know this makes absolutely no sense on an intellectual level, yet we do it anyway. What we need, then, is to bring the saboteur out into the light, confront it, and change its job description to "encourager." Once we do that, we can reintegrate it back into our decision-making process and use it for good.

Seems Like a Friend, Acts Like a Foe

If you want to overcome your inner saboteur, you first need to realize that you may *say* you want one thing, but your actions reveal that you want something else. Maybe it will help to think of your inner saboteur as a self-created safety mechanism that steps in to protect you whenever you might be putting yourself in danger. Many fears that people wrestle with become opportunities for the saboteur to do its nasty work. For example, many of us fear rejection, failure, humiliation, and loss of control, but did you know that some people fear success, intimacy, and love? More specifically, they fear they will attain these things only to lose them eventually, so they think, *Why bother? I will only be embarrassed and hurt when it all comes crashing down.* When we feel overwhelmed, lack confidence, or struggle to make certain things right in our life, we call on the inner saboteur to stop us from putting forth any effort that might get us to a place where we risk losing what we've worked for. In Josh's mind, the risks of being rejected outweighed the possible rewards of a loving and lasting relationship with a young woman who shared his interests. I'm sure you can see how this mindset is self-defeating and unproductive.

To see another example of the sneaky saboteur in action, let's take a look at Lany's story. Ever since she was a little girl, Lany dreamed of playing basketball in college, going pro after graduation, and representing her country proudly in the Olympics. During middle school, Lany was an average player. Short, timid, and very uncoordinated, she never started and only occasionally scored a few points. Her freshman year she barely made the team and almost never played. Nevertheless, Lany kept hitting the gym and playing pickup whenever she could, still hoping one day she would reach her goals. Unfortunately, sophomore year wasn't a whole lot better than her freshman year. Lany made the team, and she played and scored more than before, but still she did not stand out.

But then something happened the summer before Lany's junior year. After years of hard work and dedication, Lany's game finally started to click. Her jump shot took form, her dribble became unstoppable, and her defense was menacing to other teams. It didn't hurt that Lany grew a couple of inches that summer, but it also didn't matter. Lany's game was getting stronger and stronger by the week, and her prospects looked brighter and brighter.

During her junior year, Lany absolutely dominated her competition. She went from single-digit minutes and single-digit scoring to starting full time and scoring 25 points per game. Led by Lany's dominant play and natural leadership skills, her team started the season strong, and by the time they were 10-0, people began to take notice. Lany went from having no fans to having her own cheering section. She made national news one night when she single-handedly brought her team back from a 12-point deficit in the last 90 seconds and hit a game-winning three-pointer at the buzzer. Midway through the season the college recruitment letters began to pour in, and by the end she was named team MVP, district scoring champion, and recipient of Conference Athlete of the Year by her local newspaper. Lany's team placed third in the state tournament, and Lany was named All-State Player of the Year Honorable Mention. Finally, it looked like Lany's goals might be becoming a reality, but it wouldn't be long before her inner saboteur would make an appearance and her success would take an awful turn.

While Lany loved playing basketball at the level she always knew she could, she hated the spotlight. Having her mom at the game was one thing; having a whole cheering section was another thing entirely. Lany was a bit shy normally, so when she was interviewed for newspaper articles or local TV shows, or when she was introduced to college recruiters and asked about her life, plans, and goals, Lany froze. Also, Lany began to feel a lot of pressure to perform at a high level. It wasn't a big deal when Lany scored five points per game in middle school or when she went 0 for 10 from the line her freshman year, but things were different now. Lany was becoming a local star with real national potential. Everywhere she went people stopped her and asked all kinds of questions about her training, how she would help her team win state next year, and even which college she planned to commit to. People expected big things from Lany, and failure was not an option.

Despite the fact that her game had never been stronger, Lany began to feel very nervous heading into her final season of high school basketball. Too many people asked too many questions, and everyone's expectations—her parents', her coaches', her teammates', and even recruiters'—were high. Lany began to wilt under the pressure. Suddenly that jump shot she had worked so long to perfect was no longer dropping like it used to, her dribble was getting stolen multiple times per game, and opposing offenses moved through her defense like she wasn't even there. Her statistics slipped badly, and her team, which everyone favored to win state that year, got off to a terrible start, winning only four of their first ten games. By midseason Lany was no longer starting, and by season's end she was sitting on the end of the bench in street clothes, faking a torn hamstring she claimed she sustained working out at home.

Lany's team didn't make the state tournament her senior year, and she received no official offers from any of the colleges that were looking at her the year before.

I met Lany several years after she graduated high school. After her senior season she never played basketball again. No college, no pro league, and no Olympics. In fact, Lany didn't even play pickup ball in her neighborhood anymore because she didn't want people to see her playing and have to explain what had happened to her career. In therapy Lany confided to me that she had never told anyone that she faked her injury and that she had been carrying the shame and embarrassment over this secret for years. When I asked Lany what she thought had caused her downfall, she responded, "I don't really know. I just felt that so many people had such high expectations for me that I didn't think I could ever meet them. Even though I worked hard, I still felt like I wasn't good enough, like my success wasn't real and that any minute everyone would realize I wasn't the player they thought I was. I figured there was no way I would *actually* accomplish my goals and that ultimately I would fail anyway. I just got in my own head so much that I convinced myself I wouldn't succeed, so I gave up to avoid the pressure." In other words, she had met, and been defeated by, her inner saboteur.

Josh and Lany aren't the only ones who shoot themselves in the foot when confronting something they fear. Dave was so hurt by a girlfriend who cheated on him during senior year that he avoided all women for the next decade—just to prevent the possibility of being hurt again. As a result, Dave's self-imposed isolation has caused him to become lonely and bitter, not to mention completely unskilled at talking to women who might have been a good match for him. Jack was the envy of all his friends when he started a successful photography business right after college, but his business failed after just a few short months due to circumstances largely out of his control. To avoid feeling the embarrassment he felt the day he told his friends that his business was closing,

Jack pretends that he has no ambition and doesn't care about success in business. Jack's saboteur has convinced him that it's better to look like a slacker than a failure, so he doesn't even try. And Stephanie's parents were professional pianists who trained her to carry on the family tradition. Confident that she would never be as talented a pianist as her parents and convinced that she would embarrass them—and herself—for her perceived lack of talent, Stephanie refused to practice at all and started telling her parents, "Piano is lame anyway." As a result, Stephanie's relationship with her parents has suffered somewhat over the years, and she squandered a rare opportunity to develop real talent under the tutelage of professionals who love her.

In each of these cases, it should be clear who the culprit is. You see, your inner saboteur *thrives* during times of conflict, undermining your success by convincing you you're not good enough, not smart enough, or not worthy of real happiness or success. The saboteur reminds you of your previous traumas and mistakes and, in order to protect you from the embarrassment or shame of experiencing them again, convinces you that what you're after will only cause you more harm in the end. Dave didn't want to be single; he just didn't want to be hurt again. Jack didn't want to be a professional slacker; he just didn't want to fail at business again. And Stephanie didn't want to quit piano and hurt her parents' feelings; she just wanted to avoid the possibility of not living up to their successes. Recognizing that you self-sabotage is one thing, but how exactly do you put your saboteur back in its place without killing it entirely?

CONTROL YOUR SABOTEUR

At this point it should be fairly clear that self-sabotage is really just an act of protection and self-preservation. But it should also be clear that this excessive caution may be the very thing holding you back from reaching your goals and finding your happiness. The saboteur is sneaky and clever, and it uses your fears to manipulate you into acting against your own self-interests, but you make things worse when you ignore or excuse self-destructive or counterproductive behavior. Next time you hear that little voice telling you to be cautious or not take healthy risks, try to retain the positive benefits of self-protection while pushing through the self-defeating tendency to avoid risk entirely. The following five steps will help make that easier.

1. Embrace the Saboteur

Your inner saboteur is like your big brother who protects you from schoolyard bullies, but who also sometimes protects you so much that he prevents you from making friends. It is not something you want to eliminate from your life entirely, but you definitely should know when to use it and when to ignore it. The impulse to protect yourself from things you fear is part of your survival instinct. If your ancestors hadn't had it they would have been tasty snacks for very large predators. But somewhere along the way your inner saboteur became separated from who you are and what you really need to thrive. Embrace your saboteur as your inner protector from the things you fear, but be wary of which fears are all in your head and which ones are real. Your saboteur takes its lead from you, so you need to confide in it what really matters to you and what you need to do to accomplish your goals. By embracing your saboteur, you will begin to recognize the ways it seeks to protect you by causing you to act in ways that are against your self-interest.

2. Address Your Fear

To address the saboteur, you must first identify precisely what it is fighting. What, exactly, do you fear, and what does this fear say about you? If you're afraid of failure or intimacy or even success, try to understand where that fear came from. Then rethink who you are and what you're capable of becoming. You no longer have to accept or engage in your self-defeating behaviors. It's okay to be scared, and it's okay to be angry, but the sooner you figure out what is causing these feelings—and what they're preventing you from accomplishing—the sooner you will be able to move past them and focus your energy on accomplishing your goals.

3. Create a New Game Plan

If you want your life to be different, you cannot continue to operate as you always have. Once you recognize how and why the saboteur presents itself, you need to be realistic about what you must do differently. For instance, is your fear of intimacy—or, more precisely, of *losing* intimacy—causing you to avoid pursuing romantic relationships? Avoiding what you fear will only cause more fear, so go after what you want—even if you fail a few times along the way. It may not feel like it at the time, but every time you fail at something, you're growing closer to success. Reflection on your failures and mistakes becomes a source of wisdom when you learn from them and adapt accordingly. Michael Jordan was famously cut from his high school's basketball team when he was in tenth grade. Perhaps if Lany had followed his example instead of listening to her inner saboteur she might be the proud owner of a few very heavy pieces of gold-plated jewelry. The bottom line: Come up with a game plan that you can follow the next time your inner saboteur tells you to take a step back. Determine what matters and how you will accomplish it. Against determination and a well-laid plan, your inner saboteur doesn't stand a chance.

4. Work Your Plan

A plan that gathers dust is no plan at all. To reach your goals, you must implement your plan. But when you do, be sure to include your inner saboteur. Since you can't ignore it completely—nor should you—you should reframe its role to suit your purposes. For example, Connor was a talented law school grad working for his first big firm, but he had an irrational fear of looking foolish in front of his more-seasoned colleagues that prevented him from speaking out in important meetings. Connor recognized that his fear would prevent him from moving up in the firm, so before each meeting he reinforced his positive self-image by reminding himself that his legal expertise and outspokenness were what gave his bosses the confidence they needed to hire him in the first place. Connor also recognized that sometimes he might fail— that he might sometimes say things in a meeting that his bosses would dismiss—but that these failures were not signs that he wasn't talented as a lawyer; they were signs that he was taking risks and being assertive toward his goals. Now instead of letting his saboteur convince him to be quiet in meetings, Connor recognizes it as a sign that he is simply nervous, and he quietly convinces himself that everything will be fine as he converses confidently with his superiors.

5. Thrive

The last step to keeping your saboteur in check and not allowing it to prevent you from accomplishing your goals is to resolve to always keep moving forward in a positive direction, even if things sometimes don't go according to plan. Maintaining a positive attitude in the face of setbacks keeps the saboteur from doing any real or permanent damage. Too often, people embark on a new life plan, suffer a setback, and allow this setback to color all aspects of their self-image. You may have failed your math test, but this does not make you a failure. As long as you recognize that you are intelligent, capable, and courageous enough to take a risk—and resilient enough to get back up if things don't go well—your saboteur can't harm you through self-destructive behavior.

When you do fail at something, use positive reinforcement to get back on your feet. For example, tell yourself things like, *My team may have lost, but I played my hardest,* or, *I may have been rejected by one guy, but that does not make me unworthy or undeserving of love.* Remember, your perception is reality. If you perceive a setback to be permanent, it will be. If you perceive it to be a learning experience, it will be that instead. The most important thing about any situation is how you respond to it, so respond in a way that will help you move forward positively.

Whether it's at home, work, school, or in a relationship, figure out when you're most likely to sabotage yourself. When these situations arise, implement these five steps immediately. The more you practice them, the sooner they will become second nature. Taking risks can be scary, but as you begin to discover how these five steps can prevent you from engaging in self-destructive behavior—or from avoiding behaviors that will help you accomplish your goals—you will be that much more motivated to embrace your fears and move proactively toward your goals.

Now let's try some exercises that will help you deal with
your internal saboteur in positive ways.

———

EXERCISES

In this chapter, we've introduced you to that sneaky little monster who lives in your head and tries to talk you out of taking healthy risks. The bad news is your inner saboteur is never going away for good, but the good news is you can use what it's telling you to your advantage. The following exercises are designed to help you recognize when it is most likely to rear its ugly head and what you can do next time it does.

① Take Inventory of Your Inner Saboteur

The following questions are designed to help you determine how your saboteur operates. This identification
process is important because the more you know about
your saboteur, the better you'll be at managing it.
Check all answers that apply to you.

What does your saboteur keep you from achieving?

_____ academic or professional success

_____ satisfying relationships with others

_____ spending time on hobbies and activities

_____ other _____

When does your saboteur appear?

_____ when you're under a great deal of stress

_____ when you're afraid or angry

_____ when you're on the cusp of achieving a goal
or starting to feel really good about yourself

_____ other _____

What, exactly, do you fear?

_____ academic or professional failure

_____ being hurt when someone leaves me

_____ being responsible for something I can't maintain

_____ other _____

Where did this fear originate?

_____ trauma from my childhood

_____ feeling like a failure during previous experiences

_____ seeing others fail at things I hope to accomplish

_____ other _____

2 What's the Worst that Could Happen?

People have a tendency to imagine a catastrophe where there is merely fear or discomfort. This exercise is designed to help you confront the worst possible outcome, to recognize that it's not as horrible as you think, and to move past it when it does arise.

Considering what you fear the most, describe what you think the worst possible outcome of this fear would be.

_____

_____

_____

_____

_____

_____

Has this worst possible outcome ever happened? If not, what is the worst thing that has happened, and how far removed is it from your worst fear?

_____

_____

_____

_____

_____

_____

Now imagine for a moment that your worst-case outcome actually happens one day. Describe three ways you could respond that would minimize the damage and help you move forward in a positive way.

1. _____

_____

2. _____

_____

3. _____

_____

3 The Five Steps

With the previous exercise in mind, you are now ready to put the five steps discussed in this chapter into action. By now you should know that your saboteur is trying to protect you from something that probably isn't as awful as you have feared. With this in mind, take the following steps.

1. Embrace the Saboteur

Write a statement acknowledging what the saboteur is trying to do for you. In other words, identify the saboteur's motives and embrace its function in your life.

I recognize that my inner saboteur _____

_____

_____

_____

_____

_____

_____

_____

_____

_____

_____

_____

_____

2. Address Your Fear

Now that you understand why the saboteur acts as it does, write a positive statement describing what you would like it to do instead of causing you to run from your fears.

Next time my inner saboteur appears, I would like it to help me _____

_____

_____

_____

_____

_____

3. Create a New Game Plan

Now that you know why your saboteur appears and what you fear, create a new strategy for accomplishing your goals. What, specifically, will you do differently to help you move forward in a positive direction?

To help myself accomplish my goals, I will _____

_____

_____

_____

_____

_____

4. Work Your Plan

Now that you have a plan in place, how, exactly, will you ensure your plan is carried out next time you're afraid of failure? Describe what you will do or say to yourself next time your inner saboteur tries to prevent you from accomplishing your goals.

Next time my saboteur tries to prevent me from accomplishing my goals, I will

_____

_____

_____

_____

_____

_____

5. Thrive

Next time you try something and it doesn't work out exactly the way you had hoped it would, how will you bounce back? Describe what you will do or say to yourself to make sure that your failures become successes instead of permanent roadblocks.

Next time I fail at something, I will bounce back by _____

_____

_____

_____

_____

_____

Envision Your Success

Now that you've created a game plan for handling your
inner saboteur next time it rears its ugly head, describe all
of the success you will achieve by acting proactively and
without fear toward accomplishing your specific goals.

Now that I have conquered my inner saboteur, I will _____

_____

_____

_____

_____

_____

_____

_____

_____

_____

_____

_____

_____

_____

_____

_____

TRUTH N°5

TRUTH N° 5

All Behavior Requires Permission, so You Must Learn What You're Permitting Yourself to Do

If you are sometimes confused by your own actions, you are not alone. We all do things we sometimes can't explain, but believe it or not, before every action you take, you give yourself permission to act. Now wait a second, I know what you're thinking: *But Dr. Cortman, I didn't give myself permission to smack my little brother. I just sorta did it without thinking.* On one level you're right: You probably did do it without thinking. But on another level you're wrong: Whether you realize it or not, somewhere between the moment you felt the impulse to smack him and the moment your mean old hand met his sweet little face, you decided that hitting your brother was an acceptable thing to do. Social Black Belt Truth N°5 examines the fact that all human behavior requires permission. This chapter will help you gain control over your actions by examining the ways you give yourself permission to act—even when you don't realize you're doing it—and will help you develop strategies for developing better patterns of behavior.

Carlos was 19 and home from college for a long weekend with his family. On his second night home, he walked into his 14-year-old sister's bedroom and touched her sexually while she slept. She woke up during Carlos' attack, pushed him away, and ran to her parents' room to tell them what happened. His parents were furious, but they did not call the police. Instead, Carlos left the next morning before his family awoke, and they have not spoken to him since.

It is completely normal for a young man to be sexually attracted to a young woman and to want to touch her, but several factors make Carlos' sexual act an egregious violation of social and moral norms. First, the young woman he touched is his sister. For multiple reasons, incest is socially taboo and criminally outlawed in America.

Second, the young woman is just that—a young woman. Sex with someone his sister's age violates laws in every state. Third, Carlos' sister did not consent to being touched. Without verbal consent, Carlos' sexual act is actually sexual assault, another crime. These three factors make Carlos' exploitation of his sister entirely unacceptable and illegal on several levels.

Before this event, Carlos was a decent man, and since then he has been the same. So how could an otherwise good person commit such a horrible act? When I asked Carlos this question, his response was, "I really don't know, Dr. Cortman. It sorta just... happened." The real answer, however, is that on some level Carlos gave himself permission to sexually assault his younger sister.

Let me give you another example from my own life. When I was a younger man and the world was in black and white, I once received a speeding ticket for driving 50 miles per hour in a 35 mile-per-hour zone. Naturally, I was quite upset. But instead of accepting responsibility for my actions, I came up with every excuse in the book. "The cop pulled me over because of my red convertible." "The cop was just looking to fill his monthly quota." "I was running late." "Thirty-five on that road is too slow anyway." "I'm a good driver, so I should be allowed to go faster than the speed limit." And on and on and on.

For six weeks I fumed to anyone who would listen about stupid laws, corrupt police officers, and the absolute unfairness of a cold, cruel universe *definitely* out to make the life of a young Chris Cortman infinitely miserable. Never once did it cross my mind that the ticket was simply my fault and that I deserved it for breaking the law.

To save a little money on my ticket and to avoid costly points on my driving record, I elected to attend driver safety school one Saturday afternoon. Already feeling bitter about the injustice of my ticket and supremely ticked off about being forced to give up my day off for a stupid driving class (which wasn't actually true, given that I *chose* to attend the class), I sat at the back of the room with a scowl on my face and the intention to argue my case about the injustices of the world to anyone who would listen. Instead, I met an instructor who told me the last thing I *wanted* to hear but the one thing I *needed* to hear—that I received the ticket for speeding because I gave myself permission to speed, plain and simple. And he was right. The fact of the matter was that I *had* given myself permission to speed. Sure, I was running late. And sure, the reason I was running late wasn't actually my fault. But those details still did not give me the right to break the law. I knew the speed limit, and I knew that I was exceeding it. And I also knew the potential consequences of getting pulled over. Yet despite knowing all these crucial bits of information, I sped anyway. I may not have been thinking these things while I was driving, but on a subconscious level I know them every time I get into my car and start the engine. No excuses, no one else's fault. I, Chris Cortman, victim of only my own bad decisions, gave myself permission to break the law and deserved to be punished for it.

Thankfully, I learned a hard lesson that day, and I have been a responsible driver ever since. You can do the same today. The sooner you understand Social Black Belt Truth N°5—that you behave the way you do *because you give yourself permission to*—the sooner you will regain control over your actions and have better experiences overall.

Behavior Doesn't Just Happen

Try this experiment: Think back to when you were very young and you first learned the basic differences between good and bad, right and wrong. Is stealing right or wrong? Is disrespecting your parents or teachers good or bad? Is it okay to lie? For most people, these lessons are internalized early in life—before age 8 or so. Of course, simply *knowing* right from wrong doesn't necessarily mean you will always make right choices. If you're like most people, you will struggle to make good moral decisions until the day you die. For example, your girlfriend says she loves you, but you're not quite sure how you feel yet. On the one hand, you don't want to hurt her feelings by not saying you love her, but on the other hand you don't want to lie to her and say you do if you're not really sure that's how you feel. Here's another example. Your best friend offers you a job at the fast-food restaurant she manages. On the one hand you really need the job and want to work with your friend. On the other hand, you're a vegetarian and think the fast-food industry is immoral for its mistreatment and slaughter of animals. So what do you do? Do you lie to spare someone's feelings, only to maybe hurt them much worse later on when you confess you never loved her to begin with? Do you take a job that violates your moral convictions just for a weekly paycheck? Sometimes these decisions are very difficult.

As you can see, making moral decisions is rarely black and white, and it's hard to come up with a set of rules that governs your behavior in all situations. In all cases, though, the facts remain that you have choices and that no matter what you choose to do, you first must give yourself permission to do it.

Sometimes we grant ourselves permission to do things we previously did not. When this happens, problem behaviors begin. Take using marijuana for example.

Marijuana is considered a gateway drug because many people—though certainly not all—begin using more dangerous drugs after they've begun using it. When they use marijuana for the first time, a psychological boundary has been crossed. What was once impermissible—using mind-altering drugs—has become permissible. Almost no one's first drug experience is shooting heroin, but once permission has been granted to take one drug, permission is more readily granted to using other, harder drugs. The great leap, then, isn't going from using marijuana to cocaine or from using cocaine to crack; it's from not using drugs at all to using some—even marijuana. Needless to say, the use of any drug requires permission from the self.

Drug use isn't the only problem behavior that requires permission from the self. Contrary to the excuses people make, cheating on one's boyfriend or girlfriend doesn't "just happen." Infidelity involves a series of activities that *all* require permission from the self. Flirting with a stranger is a *choice*. Trading phone numbers or social media information is a *choice*. Making plans to meet up secretly is a *choice*. Having physical relations with someone other than your significant other is a *choice*. Lying about where you were and who you were with is a *choice*. None of this stuff is out of your control. Engaging in any of this behavior is a choice that requires permission.

Violence is another problem behavior that requires self-granted permission. For many people, the impulse that many people have toward solving problems with fists (or worse) is deeply rooted in lessons about masculinity that many people learn in childhood from their parents, their peers, and society. Unfortunately, many people are taught as children that violence *does* solve problems, and they continue to practice these backward lessons as adults, often teaching their own children the same poisonous ideas they were taught. Children who are abused often grow up to abuse children of their own.

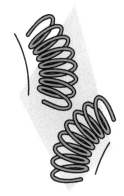

Boys who saw their fathers beat their mothers often grow up to do the same to their girlfriends and wives. In fact, some young men are *explicitly* taught that the best way to teach a woman a lesson is to beat her. How awful! But even though most lessons about violence were learned in the distant past, each subsequent act of violence requires a granting of permission from the self.

One of my patients recently confessed to me that his wife sometimes hits him when they argue. When I explained to him that this is spousal abuse and a crime, he excused her behavior by saying she only does it when she's really angry, and besides, she's a good woman who treats him well most of the time. Plus, she never really *hurts* him— not on the outside, at least. But everything about this situation is wrong. My patient's wife should definitely not be hitting her husband, even when she's angry, yet she gives herself permission to do it.

Unfortunately, many people abuse their spouses and significant others at home, yet these same people never raise a hand to their bosses, friends, or strangers in public. Why not? Because they haven't given themselves permission to. On the other hand, most people never raise their hands to anyone—not their spouses, children, pets, neighbors, or even strangers. And why not? Because they haven't given themselves permission to hit *anyone*.

Fortunately, these ideas about solving problems with violence are being exposed for what they are: outdated, toxic, and wrong. All across the country, anger management programs teach abusers to be mindful of the thought patterns that lead to acts of violence. They are taught to examine their attitudes about violence and where they developed these ideas. When people think things like, *I will slap the crap out of her if she disrespects me one more time*, they are encouraged to remind themselves that this impulse will not solve their problems and will likely lead to even worse problems in the future. Then they are taught to initiate alternative problem-solving strategies like imagining the consequences of their actions: injuring themselves or others, going to jail, hurting their friends and loved ones, or losing job and scholarship opportunities. To act violently requires permission. To act nonviolently does as well. Do yourself and everyone else a favor: Grant yourself permission to stop the cycle of abuse. Violence solves nothing and most often only makes matters much, much worse.

Of course, not every misbehavior is criminal or violent. For example, have you ever been rude or disrespectful to your parents or teachers? Have you ever said something mean or nasty to someone who didn't deserve it? Have you ever mouthed off when a person of authority asked you to do something? Of course you have, and so have I. The truth is, we all sometimes mistreat others who don't deserve it, but this, too, requires permission. No one, including you, enjoys or appreciates being disrespected, so you shouldn't do it to others. I'm sure you've heard the Golden Rule a million times—Treat others the way you want to be treated—but there's a reason it's been around for thousands of years: If you don't like the feeling of others mistreating you, don't do it to them. Violence breeds violence, and hatred breeds hatred. But, kindness and love breed kindness and love. Just as you wouldn't give someone else permission to yell at you, insult you, or treat you unkindly, you must also deny yourself permission to do it to them. Next time you want to talk back to your parents or talk trash to someone at school, just don't. It may not always be easy, but being a nice person—even to people who may not always be very nice to you—just feels better and makes life much easier. No one likes drama, and no one likes disrespect, so give yourself permission to be a better person. Trust me, your relationships and your life will improve just by being a little bit nicer next time.

The other side of that coin, of course, is that sometimes people mistreat or disrespect you for no good reason at all. One way to respond, of course, is to snap right back—to hurl an insult or throw a punch. Another is to say nothing and allow it to continue. But there is a third option: to either verbalize that the mistreatment you are receiving is unacceptable to you or to remove yourself from the situation. When you don't do these things—when you allow others to tease you, steal from you, cheat on you, or mistreat you in other ways—your silence and inaction

tell others that they have *permission* to treat you however they want. Some people are very good at standing up for themselves by letting others know right away that these forms of disrespect will not be tolerated. For many, however, denying others permission to mistreat them is quite difficult. Unfortunately, when you allow this kind of behavior to continue, you are telling your abuser, "Go ahead, I give you permission to treat me however you want."

Instead, give others permission to treat you with only love and kindness. Give others permission to treat you with respect and consideration. Tell them that, since you will always strive to treat them with love and respect, courtesy and consideration, you expect them to treat you the same way. It may be hard at first to be assertive and stand up for yourself, but next time you feel yourself being mistreated, kindly remind the other person that they do not have permission to do that to you. You will be pleased with the results.

Permission to Change

Just as your current behavior—drinking, unsafe sex, lying to your parents, or whatever—requires self-granted permission, changing your behavior for the better also requires permission. If you don't grant yourself permission to think, act, and speak differently, guess what? You won't. As the old saying goes, if nothing changes, nothing changes. Without an honest assessment of exactly what you must do to improve yourself and your relationships, you will keep falling back into your old routines, no matter how negative the results may be. Do you *really* need to become a drug addict before you'll grant yourself permission to stop experimenting with drugs? Do you *really* need to go to jail before you'll give yourself permission to stop shoplifting? Do you need to fail your class or lose your best friend before you'll give yourself permission to try harder at school or stop spreading rumors? You're no dummy. You know the results of certain negative behaviors already. You've seen the drunk-driving deaths on the news. You've seen your neighbors or relatives struggle with addiction. You've seen good people make really bad decisions and pay very high prices—sometimes the ultimate price. Unless you want to end up the same way, think about what you're doing, *stop giving yourself permission to do it*, and make a plan to change your ways. Telling yourself, "Let's just see how it goes" will not get it done. Unless you make a firm commitment to stop doing the bad stuff and start doing the good stuff, you're likely to end up in a very bad place. A new path forward means first giving yourself permission to change. Let's take a look at how you can do that.

GIVE YOURSELF PERMISSION TO CHANGE

Changing your behaviors is not as simple as snapping your fingers and saying, "I no longer give myself permission to do bad stuff." As anyone who has ever tried to quit an addiction or begin an exercise routine knows, changing is always easier said than done. For this reason, it helps to have a process in place to give yourself *real* permission to change. Use the following six steps to help you.

1. Identify the problem

This may seem like a no brainer, but you can't change a problem behavior if you aren't even aware it's a problem. Would you add gas to your tank if you didn't think it was empty? Would you stop drinking soda if you didn't know it was bad for you? Obviously you already know your car needs gas to run and that soda is unhealthy, but wouldn't it be better to fix these problems *before* you're stranded on the side of the road or 100 pounds over-weight? Permanently changing your problem behaviors will be a lot easier if you recognize your problems before they get too far out of control. Too many people are in prison or the grave because they waited just a little too long to get help. If you're not sure if you have a problem, talk to your friends, family, teachers, guidance counselor—in other words, anyone you trust. Ask them for an honest assessment of what they've observed. Odds are they will be able to identify a problem behavior, even if you can't. It's like having bad breath—you might think you've got that fresh-from-the-dentist smell, but if everyone around you is plugging their noses when you talk, maybe they're smelling something you can't. Whether you already know you have a problem, or you need a trusted person to give you a little heads up, identifying your problem behavior sooner rather than later will make correcting it that much easier.

2. Commit to Change

Here is where you stop giving yourself permission to con-tinue your destructive behavior and start giving yourself permission to engage in positive behavior. Tell yourself you are no longer allowed to play video games all week-end and eat an entire bag of chips every night before bed. You are no longer allowed to flirt with other girls. You are no longer allowed to steal jewelry from the mall. What-ever it is you've been getting into, tell yourself you are just not allowed to do that anymore. Instead, tell yourself you *are* allowed to exercise and have a healthy snack when you're hungry. You *are* allowed to treat your significant other with respect. And you *are* allowed to pay for things, just like everyone else. Easy, right? Wrong! There's a catch: When you give yourself permission to stop a bad behavior and start a good one, *you actually have to mean it.* I can tell myself a million times that I'm going to climb Mount Everest, but until I buy myself some hiking boots and book a flight to Nepal, my words are meaningless. And you can't just say you'll "see how it goes." You have to be committed. No commitment, no change. No change—well, you already know the rest.

———

3. Establish a SMART Goal

After you've identified a problem behavior and committed to making a change, you next need to establish what you'd like to do instead. Do you want to go back to school to finish your degree? Do you want to quit smoking e-cigarettes because you realize how unhealthy and uncool they really are? How about repairing your relationship with your best friend after that big fight last month? Whatever your goal, it has to be a SMART one.

SMART is an acronym that stands for

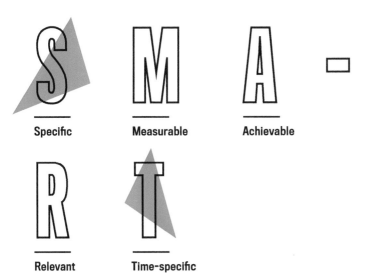

Specific   **Measurable**   **Achievable**

Relevant   **Time-specific**

Let's say this is your goal: "I want to get back in shape."
Sounds SMART, right? Wrong. So much is missing here.
What does "get back in shape" even mean? When will
you start? How will you know you've reached your goal?
Is the goal you've set for yourself even possible to begin
with? Let's see what that goal looks like the **SMART** way.

SPECIFIC

Vague goals will get you vague results, so be **specific**:
"I want to improve my diet and my level of physical fitness"
is much better than saying you want to get in shape.
Everyone wants to get in shape, but that means different
things for different people. For some people getting in
shape means losing 200 pounds. For others it means ton-
ing up for a bodybuilding competition. Think about what
you need in your life, and set a specific goal.

MEASURABLE

Make sure your goal is **measurable**: "I will know I have
reached my goal if I have gone 30 days without drinking
a soda, have lost 25 pounds, and can run a mile without
stopping" is something you will actually *know* you have
accomplished. Think about what you need to do and how
you will measure success.

ACHIEVABLE

Set a goal that is **achievable**. A man in his 80s who says
he wants to play professional football is not being realistic. A girl who says she wants to swim across the Pacific
Ocean is not being realistic. You will not do yourself any
good by setting goals you are destined not to reach, so
pick a goal within your grasp and *go after it*. Improve
your diet. Stop smoking. Talk to your best friend. Only
you know what you need to do to make your life better,
but don't set yourself up for failure before you even begin
by being unrealistic about what you want to accomplish.

RELEVANT

It may seem obvious, but make sure your goal is **relevant** to your life. What good is setting a goal to be a lawyer if you have no interest in studying law? Why tell yourself you're going to cut back on social media use if you don't even have an account? Think about what really matters to *your* life—not someone else's—and set your goals accordingly.

TIME

Set a specific **time** horizon for your goal. Will you accomplish your fitness goals in three months or six? Will you finish your degree in four years or five? Will you talk to your best friend about that fight you had this weekend or next? Only you know how urgent your issues are, but keep in mind that no one has forever. A heroin addict who says she'll kick the habit five years from now probably doesn't have that much time to spare. The longer you wait to get started, and the less specific you are about when you want to have your goals accomplished, the less likely you are to reach them.

Having a SMART goal in place lays the groundwork for giving yourself permission to make positive changes in your life. Without one, all you really have to rely on is dumb luck.

---

4. Develop a Plan

Now that you have a SMART goal like improving your diet and level of physical fitness—as opposed to just "getting in shape"—you have to develop a plan of action. Those veggies will not eat themselves, and those extra pounds don't just fall off in the shower. Will you run three days a week or five? Before school or after? And for how long? Ten minutes per day or 30? Will you join a gym? If so, which one, and how will you get there? Will you go by

yourself or with your brother, your mom, or your boy-friend? And how about that junk food? Will you eliminate all sodas and candy bars immediately, or will you cut your consumption a little more gradually? What kind of vegetables and healthy snacks will you work into your diet that you've never tried before? And how about that screen time? Seriously, how about that screen time? No one ever got in shape watching movies all day. I don't want to overwhelm you, but I think you get the point. A goal without a plan is a wish, and no one ever accomplished their goals just by wishing they would come true.

5. Work the Plan

A plan is only as good as your ability and willingness to execute it, and the reality is that many people do not accomplish their goals because they don't follow through with their plans. You could sit for hours and write out a killer diet and exercise regimen, but if you never get your lazy butt off the couch, your plan is worthless. We all know that human nature and life's obstacles often get in the way of even the best intentions. If you set a goal and fail to execute, don't give up forever. Just try again. Studies show that the more you persevere toward a goal, the more likely you are to accomplish it. For example, who's more likely to get that college degree, the person who drops out and never goes back, or the person who drops out but re-enrolls a couple semesters later?

I have a close friend who has been working on his business degree for 17 years, something the average person accomplishes in four or five. People have been telling him to give up for a long time, but he never does. Despite having a family, a full-time job, and a small side business to keep him very busy, every semester he takes a class at the local university so he is that much closer to reaching his goal. If he had dropped out when life had gotten hectic and when people told him to quit, he would not be where he is today: a mere four classes away from accomplishing his goal. The point, as Winston Churchill once said, is to "never, never, never, never... give in."

6. Alter the Routine

You've probably heard that insanity is doing the same thing over and over again and expecting different results. Although this is not a medical definition, the point is easily understood. Only an insane person would think they can get sober by having a few drinks every night, right? You probably have a friend who goes through a routine like this with her boyfriend. Fight, break up, get back together. Fight, break up, get back together. Fight, break up... ugh, it's exhausting just to think about. Crazy, right?

Here's the thing: It's almost always easier to see the crazy in everyone else than it is to see the crazy in ourselves. If you really want to experience permanent changes in your life, you have to try new things. If the old ways aren't working, change them. If your first plan didn't work out, come up with a new one. Eventually you will land on something that really gets the job done, and I think you'll be happy with the results.

New Horizons

Let me leave you with one final example of someone who had been giving himself permission to do some pretty terrible things to others but who dedicated himself to change by taking that permission away and following the six steps.

Julian came to me after being arrested at school. He was charged with assault for breaking another student's nose and cheekbone in a violent sneak attack in the stairwell. This was not Julian's first arrest; he had been beating people up in and out of school since kindergarten. So, in addition to paying the other student's medical bills and spending two years on probation, Julian was ordered to attend six months of anger-management counseling sessions with me. The judge told Julian if he failed to show significant progress in therapy, he would have his probation revoked and would spend the remainder of those two years in juvie. Obviously Julian had a lot on the line, so his dedication to our therapy sessions was crucial.

At first, Julian was a tough client—silent, moody, often disrespectful—but after a few sessions we started to get along pretty well. With my help, Julian worked through the six steps and eventually started to make some real progress. As part of his process, I asked Julian to write the other student a letter in which he apologizes for his actions and explains what he is doing to make himself better. In addition to his description of the steps, notice in the letter how Julian acknowledges giving himself permission to be violent toward others before finally taking that permission away.

DEAR PAUL,

Let me begin this letter by saying I'm really sorry for beating you up in school. I know nothing can take away the pain I caused you and your family, and if I could say it a thousand times I would—I'm sorry, I'm sorry, I'm sorry. I really hope you can forgive me for my behavior; there's really no excuse for it. The truth is that all my life I've been hurting others—lying to them, stealing from them, and beating them up when I got angry. When I was young I used to feel bad about it, but at some point I just started allowing myself to do pretty much whatever I wanted, no matter how much I hurt others or myself. I realize now that I had no right to do what I did to you, and I never should have allowed myself to get to the point where I could seriously injure someone the way I hurt you.

As you know, I've been ordered to seek therapy for my issues and to talk about the things I've done. The truth is it's been really hard, but also really good for me. With the help of my therapist, I have realized that I have some serious anger-management issues, but I am determined to turn my life around and become a better person—a person who helps people instead of hurts them. Not only am I learning a lot about myself like why I do the things I do, I've also found new ways to channel my anger appropriately. I've taken up boxing where I learn a lot about discipline and self-control, and I recently started meditating for 15 minutes every morning before school or any time I feel myself starting to get mad. I've found that these activities really make a difference in how I feel about myself and how I handle difficult situations. It wasn't easy at first—especially the meditating (LOL)—but I stuck with it, and I'm already doing so much better. I still get really mad sometimes, but I feel really confident that if I keep seeing my therapist and working the plan we've set up for me, then I can come out of this whole situation a much better person—maybe even one you could find it in your heart to forgive.

I know I've caused you a lot of pain, and I'm really, really sorry for it. If there were some way I could go back and change that day, I would do it in a heartbeat. But I can't. I can only look forward to a future where I'm truly a changed person. In the meantime, please know that I'm working really hard to make that happen.

I hope you're feeling better. Maybe one day, if you're feeling up to it, we can talk face to face so I can apologize again in person and show you I'm not the same as I was the day I hurt you so badly.

Sincerely,

JULIAN

Here's the bottom line: You need to know your destructive behaviors and the dangerous routines that draw you into them, and remind yourself that you no longer have permission to do the things you've been doing. Instead, give yourself permission to embrace *new* behaviors and *new* patterns to disrupt your old ways. When this happens, you are on your way to a healthier, happier you.

Now let's try some exercises to help you apply Truth N°5 to your life.

———

EXERCISES

By now we hope you understand that every action you take is one that you've given yourself permission to. You should also understand that knowing right from wrong isn't that same as always doing what's right. The following exercises will help you to identify what you've been giving yourself permission to do and why and to create a plan to start heading in a different direction.

1 What Do You Give Yourself Permission to Do?

You may think you know what your negative behaviors are, but often this is not the case. Many people struggle to identify their problem behaviors, counterproductive routines, and negative patterns because they deny them or make excuses for them. This exercise is designed to help you become more aware of what might be causing some of your problems.

The following list includes some common behavior problems that you may be engaging in. While being honest with yourself is sometimes difficult, it's necessary if you want to make a clean start. Make a check mark next to any that apply to you.

_____ Sabotaging relationships with your friends, family, or significant other

_____ Becoming hostile or angry, especially when you're under stress

_____ Hurting others you care about

_____ Skipping school or not performing as well as you can

_____ Spending too much money, especially on things you don't need

_____ Worrying constantly about things you can't change

_____ Poor hygiene

_____ Poor diet and/or exercise routine

_____ Too much screen time

_____ Spreading rumors

_____ Drinking, smoking, and/or using drugs

_____ Disrespecting or rebelling against authority figures

_____ Stealing

_____ Bullying in person or online

_____ Unsafe sex

_____ Other _____

2 Why Do You Do It?

The goal of this exercise is to help you understand *why* you engage in these negative behaviors. Below are five common ways people excuse their negative behaviors so they can continue them. For each example, think of one of the items you checked in Exercise 1 and write an example of exactly how you're giving yourself permission to do it.

Rationalization

When you rationalize your behaviors, you're basically just making up an excuse or maybe even an outright lie for why you did something you shouldn't have. My favorite excuse when I was a kid was, "My dinosaur ate my homework." Write an example of how you've rationalized one of your bad behaviors.

_____

_____

_____

_____

_____

Minimization

When you minimize, you're basically admitting you've done something wrong while trying to make it seem like it's not as serious as it really is. For example, "Yeah, I ate two whole candy bars, but at least I didn't eat three!" Write an example of how you minimize something in your life.

_____

_____

_____

_____

_____

Intellectualization

When you intellectualize, you're trying to block out any emotional aspects of a situation by creating what you think is a logical argument to justify it. One of my recent patients was arrested at school for marijuana possession. He intellectualized his behavior this way: "I may smoke a lot of weed, but science has proven that marijuana is less addictive than cigarettes and less harmful than alcohol, so when you think about it, really I'm making the healthier choice." Write an example of a time when you intellectualized something you shouldn't have.

_____

_____

_____

_____

Denial

You probably already know what denial is. When you deny something, you basically say something didn't happen when really it did. When one of my patients was arrested for stealing earrings from the mall, she told the security guard and police officers, "I don't know how those earrings ended up in my pocket. I didn't steal anything." What have you denied?

_____

_____

_____

_____

_____

Externalization/Projection

When you externalize your bad behaviors, you project them onto someone or something else–in other words, you blame others for something you did. Recently, one of my patients arrived home from work several hours later than usual after taking her daughter to the emergency room. She came home to her dog crying in its cage, covered with its own feces. Her teenage son, who was upstairs playing video games the whole time, said, "The dog's Sarah's responsibility, not mine." What bad behaviors have you projected onto others?

_____

_____

_____

_____

_____

3 Give Yourself Permission to Change

Now that you've identified some of the problem
behaviors you're giving yourself permission to engage
in and the ways you make excuses for them, it's time
to decide how you're going to make a change. Answer
the following questions.

Identify the Problem

Which problem behavior from the ones selected above would you most like
to change?

_____

_____

_____

_____

Commit to Change

In the space below, write a clear statement that shows you no longer give yourself permission to engage in your problem behavior. (Example: "I commit to no
longer stealing from my mother's purse." Or "I no longer give myself permission
to cheat on my math homework.")

_____

_____

_____

_____

_____

Get SMART

Now is the time to create a goal that will help you develop new habits for positive change. Use the examples to guide you.

S: What **specific** goal would you like to accomplish? (Example: "My math grade was a C last quarter, so I would like to improve it this quarter.")

_____

_____

_____

M: How will you **measure** your success? (Example: "I will know I have accomplished my goal if I maintain an average of 80% or higher throughout the quarter and finish with a B.")

_____

_____

_____

A: Is your goal **achievable**? If not, think about creating a new goal you _can_ accomplish. If yes, write a statement about the achievability of your goal. (Example: "My goal _is_ achievable because I am normally a good math student, but I did poorly last quarter because I was lazy about my homework and missed too many classes.")

_____

_____

_____

R: Is your goal **relevant** to your life? If not, consider creating a goal that *will* have a positive impact. (Example: "Improving my math score *is* relevant to my life because I have been slacking lately, and I know I can do better. Plus, I know that doing well in school is important to my future success.")

_____

_____

_____

T: Finally, *when* will you accomplish your goal? Create a **time** horizon for accomplishing your goal. (Example: "I will begin trying harder in math right away, and I will maintain an 80% average or better throughout the entire quarter. If I do these things, I will finish with a B or better at the end of nine weeks.")

_____

_____

_____

4 Write a Letter

While this exercise is optional, it is certainly encouraged.
Think about a time when you granted yourself permission to treat another person in a way you would not want
them to treat you. This person could be your parent,
teacher, best friend, or even a complete stranger. Using
Julian's letter as a guide, first apologize. Then, explain
how you granted yourself permission to mistreat them
and how you are working to make sure it never happens
again. While you are encouraged to give this person the
letter (Imagine how good *you* would feel if someone
wrote a letter of apology to you.), you certainly don't
have to. Since everyone's situation is different, only you
will know what is truly best. Be honest and sincere, and
most importantly, show that you are willing to be better
toward them in the future.

Dear _____ ,

_____

_____

_____

_____

_____

_____

_____

_____

_____

_____

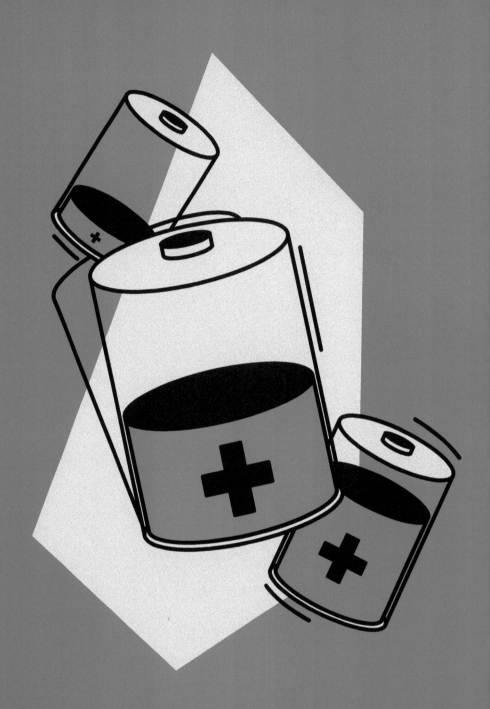

TRUTH N° 6

You Have a Limited Amount of Emotional Energy, so It Shouldn't be Wasted on Wishing, Worrying, and Whining

The careers of many professional athletes are quite short. Making it to the NFL or NBA at all is an impressive feat, but the truth is that most athletes don't last more than a few seasons. While some former pros go on to coach or find other careers in sports like broadcasting or journalism, many struggle to find new ways of spending their time when they take off their jerseys for the last time. Sadly, many develop alcohol or drug addictions or can't find work because they have few skills other than sports. But most former athletes accept that their professional sports career is over and move on to try new things. They go back to college, open businesses, and start families, for example. Instead of spending their days drinking in bars imagining they were still on the field or complaining to anyone who will listen that things should have been different or that they should have been picked up by another team, they understand that life is short and time is precious, so they don't waste their emotional energy wishing the past was different or whining about things that are out of their control.

Truth N°6 is simple. We all have a limited amount of emotional energy, so what good does it do to waste it wishing the past was different, worrying about the future or things you can't control, and whining about...well, *anything*? To be fair, we're all guilty of wishing, worrying, and whining from time to time. But when you spend your days living with regrets from the past or anger because things didn't turn out the way you wanted them to, all you are really doing is wasting more time and energy that could be spent making things better for yourself. I know this truth may seem obvious, but if you continue to wish, worry, and whine, you will only have more regrets later on.

Let's take a deeper look at how this tragic waste occurs.

Sarcastic Math— Everyone's Favorite Game!

Let's play a little game called Sarcastic Math. Think about this: How much time do you spend making excuses, complaining about things, and replaying past events or conversations you wish had turned out differently? If you're like many teenagers, the answer is probably a lot. Does any of this sound familiar? "I didn't pass my test because my teacher sucks." "Man, I *hate* waking up so early for school." "Oooh, I should've said X to her earlier; *that* would've shut her up." Unfortunately, engaging in this way of thinking accomplishes nothing more than wasting your two most precious resources: time and emotional energy. If you find yourself frequently stuck in these ruts of investing your resources in the wrong ways too often, you will probably start to feel seriously unhappy and unfulfilled—and maybe you already do.

Try to think about your available energy like a math problem—I know, I know, but I promise it won't hurt. All humans, including you, have exactly 24 hours a day to live—no more, no less. During that limited time, you also have a limited amount of emotional energy to expend. Let's pretend that your daily allotment for emotional energy is like $100. During your 24-hour day, you are free to spend that $100 worth of emotional energy however you want—it is yours, after all—but when it's spent, it's spent. You can think what you want to think, do what you want to do, and feel how you want to feel, but it all has a cost. Let's see how it goes, big baller.

You want to waste your time complaining about the blah-blah-blah so-and-so said on social media last week? That'll be $20 please. You want to spend an hour worry-ing about whether your team's going to win tomorrow instead of going outside to work on your jump shot? Yay, good times! That'll be another $20. Maybe you feel like wishing you were taller or that you had more friends. Wish away, my friend—I'm sure *that* will do the trick. Now gimme $20 more!

I'm sure you're getting the point by now, but you still have $40 worth of emotional energy to spend before the day is over—let's see how you can blow it. Hmm, maybe your little brother is annoying—most of them are, after all. You should probably have a good 30-minute fight with him over something really stupid and then complain to your mom about it for another 20. I'm sure it'll feel great! Do you hear that sound? That's your next $20 being flushed down the toilet. Phew! You must be emotionally exhausted by now, but you still have $20 to go. Hmm... what else, what else? Oh yeah, don't you just *hate* having a reasonable bedtime? I mean seriously, don't parents just suck, with their stupid rules and their blah, blah, blah, always trying to keep you safe and well-rested and set-ting you up for success? Whine, whine, whine—I need that last $20, please.

Oh, but what about that test you really need to study for or that sketch you've been meaning to get around to for the past few days? What about that college essay you've been trying to write or that talk with your boyfriend you've been putting off all week? Sorry, big spender, unfortunately you don't have any time or energy left in your emotional bank account to spend on being pro-ductive because you've been wasting it on all that other nonsense all day. At this point you are just so exhausted that all those things will have to wait until tomorrow. And so it goes, another 24 hours wasted on wishing, worrying, and whining instead of being spent productively.

Fortunately there is a better, more productive, and more emotionally satisfying way to live, one that involves focusing on the positives instead of wasting time on the negatives. Like those athletes I mentioned earlier who made for themselves rewarding lives after their careers ended, you are encouraged to have a short-term mem-ory. In other words, forget about all of the negativity that prevents you from living in the present and focus instead on all positives that will make your life better now and in the future.

Like most things, this is easier said than done, so in order to develop new habits and new ways of investing your emotional energy, you must first recognize the three most common ways people waste their emotional energy:

1. Wishing the Past Was Different

2. Worrying About the Future

3. Whining About Things You Cannot Change and Refusing to Change the Things You Can

Let's take a few minutes to look at all three of these epic time and energy wasters so you can recognize how they trespass on your thinking and then eliminate them from your life as much as possible.

1. Wishing the Past Was Different

Let me be real about one thing: We all have regrets. They're perfectly normal. For example, I regret not buying stock in Amazon and Google 20 years ago—if I had I'd be rich—but I don't spend all my precious time and energy freaking out about it. That mistake was in the past, and there's not much I can do about it today. I also regret not going to see the Beatles in concert before Lennon was killed (yes, I'm *that* old), but my time machine is broken, and I just can't go back. What's done is done, so there's no use in stressing over it.

I'm sure you have regrets too. Maybe you're in an intensive reading class this year, and you regret not trying harder in English class last year and Christmas treeing your end-of-the-year exam. Maybe you didn't make the baseball team, and you regret not taking any batting practice for six months and playing video games instead. Or maybe you're on probation, and you regret bringing all that weed to school last year. Regretting these things is completely normal. What's not normal, however, is spending all of your time and energy wishing the past was different and being unproductive in the meantime.

You have two options here: You can feel miserable and bitter every time you go to class, or you can take your work a little more seriously and try to do better this year. You can be angry or upset every time your school's team has a game, or you can support your friends who made the team and work on your swing until you're good enough to make it next season. And you can be embarrassed or more rebellious because you're on probation, or you can take your situation as a serious life lesson and vow to do better going forward.

Think about this: Are you going to be the guy who spends all his time in his room wishing he'd asked Sarah out last year before Dante asked her first, or will you take the sting from that experience and use it as motivation to be more assertive next time? Will you be the girl who's constantly bummed out and wishes she hadn't sneaked out of the house last weekend, or will you accept the fact that you deserve to be grounded and work really hard to regain your parents' trust in the meantime? The choice is all yours, my friend, but if you want my expert advice, I say the sooner you make peace with the past, the sooner you will be able to focus on what really matters in the present.

---

2. Worrying About the Future

Thinking about the future is a perfectly natural and healthy thing to do. If you didn't think about and plan for your future, you might not make good decisions today. What's not healthy, however, is worrying about things that *might* happen down the road and that you have almost no control over today. For example, it *might* rain in Mexico the week you want to go next June, but that doesn't mean you shouldn't plan a vacation. And you and your boyfriend *might* not be in a relationship forever, but that doesn't mean you shouldn't enjoy the time together now.

People tend to worry less when things are going well and worry more when things are not going so well. For example, if you had $10,000 in your savings account, how worried would you be about not being able to pay your next cell phone bill? Probably not at all. But if you had only $1 and the bill was due tomorrow, I'm guessing you probably would be.

While it is completely reasonable to be concerned about your future well-being and the well-being of your friends and family, spending lots of time constantly worrying about distant possibilities is just another harmful way of wasting your precious time and emotional energy. No one *likes* to worry, yet so many people find themselves doing it all the time. Have you ever found yourself pacing back and forth, pulling at your hair, biting your fingernails, feeling sick to your stomach, or unable to sleep at night? If so, then you were probably worried about something. Now ask yourself this: Did any of those activities actually solve any of your concerns? Did biting your nails make that cell phone money miraculously appear in your bank account? Did losing sleep worrying help your parents get approved for that car loan they desperately needed? Not at all.

The truth of the matter is that we are all sometimes— scratch that—we are *often* at the mercy of forces far beyond our control, and focusing your time and attention on things you can't control won't change those forces one bit. What's worse, all the time you spend worrying about these things is actually preventing you from dedicating time and energy to the things you *can* control right now. That 20 minutes you spent freaking out about how scary it will be to go to college four years from now was 20 minutes you didn't spend doing your homework, working out, taking a much-needed nap, straightening your hair, reading a book, volunteering at a nursing home, practicing your jump shot, or visiting your sweet old granny. And she misses you, you know.

Think about the future? Yes. Plan for the future and work your plan? Definitely. But worry excessively over it? Nah, you've got better things to do.

---

3. Whining About Things You Cannot Change And Refusing to Change the Things You Can

I live and practice psychology in Florida. Recently I conducted a very scientific poll among my patients, and the results will not surprise you: During the summer, precisely 100% of my patients walk into my office, drenched in sweat, and instantly complain about the weather. The other things they like to complain about: old people, tourists, and traffic. Oh yeah, and old people and tourists *in* traffic. My patients whine about these things so often you'd think there was a sign out front that said, "Free therapy for people who whine about things they can't do anything about." When I left work this afternoon, that sign was still not there, yet all of my patients complained about the same darned things. In fairness, they're not wrong; it *is* hot, there *are* a lot of tourists and retirees, and traffic *is* terrible—but there is literally nothing—let me repeat that—*nothing* they or I can do about it. The only things this whining has accomplished are that they continue to feel unnecessarily irritated over the weather and that they have wasted one very precious—and expensive—minute of psychotherapy with yours truly, the amazing and incomparable Dr. Cortman. That one minute whining about the heat is one minute not spent dealing with their very serious issues—suicidal thoughts, divorce, drug problems, and so on—so what's the point?

If you're like most teenagers—and I'm guessing you are (awkward, pimply, maybe a little smelly)—you probably mastered the art of whining a long time ago and could write a college essay about it. And for good reason: Somewhere along the line you learned that if you whine enough, eventually you will get what you want. Maybe whining to your parents about your curfew got you an extra half hour on the weekends, or whining about your allowance got you a little raise at the end of the week. But in reality, all of this whining, especially about things you can't control—or *could* control but don't know how to— probably gets you very little. For example, does whining about how hard your algebra class is help you understand quadratic equations any better? Will whining about how early you have to get up in the morning suddenly change the start time at your school? Or how about all that whining you do about having to share a bathroom with your brother? Did it make another toilet magically appear in your living room or make your brother disappear? I'm guessing the answers to all three of these questions is a firm no. And why would you want a bathroom in your living room anyway? That's just weird.

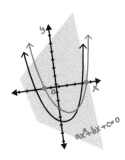

So what good does your all that whining *actually* do? The answer, as I'm sure you have already figured out, is very little. Now, this does not mean you have no right to be frustrated about things. After all, algebra *is* hard, school *does* start too early, and sharing a bathroom—especially with your smelly little brother, who pees on the seat, doesn't flush the toilet, and *never* washes his hands— *does* suck.

But if whining doesn't work, and your situation isn't ideal, what, exactly, can you do about it? Usually a lot more than you think. If you're like most of my patients and you hate the heat, you have a few options. You could wear lighter clothing, wear sunglasses and a hat to keep the sun out of your eyes and off your face, avoid going outside in the middle of the day, find an air-conditioned place to cool off, go for a swim, and drink lots of water. Or you can just suck it up and be on your sweaty way. *Complaining* about the heat, however, won't change the temperature one bit—but it will change your mindset about what could be an otherwise happy day, turning it into an unnecessarily crappy one instead.

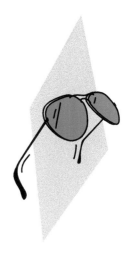

As far as math class goes, you could complain until you hate everyone and everything that breathes, or you can pay attention in class, ask questions, do your homework, and go for extra tutoring if need be. And since complaining won't change the start time at school, you could put your phone away or turn off the TV a little earlier and get some extra sleep at night so you're better rested in the morning. And as far as your bathroom situation goes—and I know you may not want to hear this—instead of complaining about it constantly and arguing with your brother every morning, you could just wake up 15 minutes earlier so you're showered and ready to go before Ol' Nasty Hands is even awake.

I know these suggestions are not ideal, but neither is doing nothing about the things you constantly whine about. And since none of these problems are going away anytime soon, the best things you can do for yourself are to adopt a more accepting attitude about the things you cannot change and to be proactive about the things you can.

Now if you'll excuse me, all this talk about whine has given me a sudden craving for some cheese.

USE YOUR ENERGY THE *RIGHT* WAY

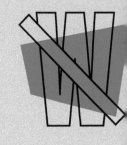

If you were to ask people if wishing, worrying, and whining are colossal wastes of resources, probably most would agree that they are. I mean really, who among us actually thinks these habits are *good* uses of energy or *effective* ways to solve problems? Probably no one, if they're being totally honest. But nevertheless, we all occasionally get caught up in painful memories of the past or the complexity and chaos at home and, as a result, find ourselves wishing, worrying, and whining uselessly about all kinds of things. But in doing so, we invest our time and energy *un*wisely, and in the end very little about what we're fretting about actually changes for the better.

On the other hand, taking Social Black Belt Truth N°6 to heart can help you monitor your ways of thinking and spend your mental energy and precious time more positively and productively. If you think and act rationally, and work toward accomplishing goals and solving problems, you will create actual changes in your life and feel better about yourself and your situations. Below are a couple ways to help you get started.

1. Accept the Things You Are Powerless to Control

The first step in 12-step programs like Alcoholics Anonymous and Narcotics Anonymous is for addicts to accept that they are "powerless over people, places, and things." Rather than causing anxiety, this admission can help you feel peace of mind knowing that there are just some things that are out of your control, so why worry about them? And even though you may not be able to control some situations, you can control how you feel about them. You can't control the weather, but you can decide to not have a bad attitude about it. You can't control traffic, but you can decide not to honk your horn like a maniac, punch the steering wheel, and flip old ladies the bird. To get the most out of this tip, next time you're in a bad situation be aware of what you can and cannot control. Then accept what is *out* of your power and take decisive action on what is *in* your power. By implementing this new thought pattern on a regular basis, you are much more likely to have a positive impact on the outcome of these situations.

2. Use Your Energy to Focus on Positive Outcomes Rather Than on Negative Thoughts

Rather than losing sleep and stressing needlessly next time you have a big game against your school's rival, think about what, exactly, you must do to improve your chances of winning—then do it. Do you need to work on defensive drills or offensive? Should you run through that trick play you've been working on with your teammates or focus on your strength and conditioning? If you have an important test coming up (they're all important, by the way), re-read your notes, do some extra practice assignments, find a study buddy, or go for extra tutoring.

Don't stress needlessly, lose precious sleep, or waste your valuable study time ignoring your curricular responsibilities. Make a plan, and make it happen. Wherever you focus your thoughts and energy, your actions will follow.

___

3. Be Conscious of How You Invest Your Energy

If your parents give you a weekly allowance or if you have a job, I'm sure you're used to keeping track of how you spend your money. If you receive $20 per week for personal spending, and you blow it all on the first day, you'll be broke as a joke for the remaining six. Try to keep track of how you're investing your energy in the same way. In other words, be mindful. Mindfulness means you must give conscious thought to how you spend your time—and how much time you spend on wishing, worrying, and whining. Every so often—maybe daily, maybe weekly or monthly—take a few quiet minutes to really think about where your thoughts and energy have been focused lately. And be honest with yourself. If it's 3 p.m., and you know you've already spent too much of the day wasting your emotional energy, it's not too late to make a change. You still have the afternoon, evening, and night to make it a great day. Here's a big word for you: *metacognition.* It means "thinking about your thinking." Every once in a while, take a minute and think about your thought patterns, and adjust them as needed. I think you'll find taking this occasional mental inventory very helpful.

BE IN THE MOMENT

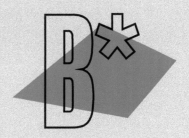

Next time you find yourself wishing, worrying, or whining, practice mindfulness by doing any of the following activities: practice meditation, do yoga, go outside and observe nature, ride your bike while listening to music that makes you happy, call (don't text) a friend or relative you haven't talked to in a while, practice a hobby you enjoy, sit quietly with a cup of tea, solve a puzzle, write poetry, or create art.

If you find yourself struggling to invest your energy wisely, don't stress it. Instead, do something positive—like the following exercises!

———

EXERCISES

We hope that by now you're starting to see how pointless it is to waste your time and energy wishing, worry, and whining. The following exercises will help you identify the situations that have been cluttering your mind, change the way you think about them, and come up with a handful of great new ways to spend all your newfound time and energy.

Before you can spend your time and emotional energy differently, you must first identify the ways in which you have been wasting them. For this exercise, take a few minutes to think about all the negative things that occupy so much of your headspace. Identifying them and getting them down on paper will help you catch yourself next time you find yourself wishing, worrying, and whining.

Past

Identify three to five things about your past that you wish were different. Write down things that leave you feeling angry, depressed, jealous, or bitter when you think about them. (Example: "I feel so angry that my father left when I was younger and never calls or comes to see me.")

1. _____

   _____

2. _____

   _____

3. _____

   _____

4. _____

   _____

5. _____

   _____

Future

Identify three to five concerns that you have about your future. Write down things that worry you, make you nervous, or keep you up at night. (Example: "I'm really scared about going off to college in two years. Who will I turn to when I'm lonely?")

1. _____

   _____

2. _____

   _____

3. _____

   _____

4. _____

   _____

5. _____

   _____

Out of Your Control

Now identify and write down three to five situations that cause you to feel angry, whiny, or nervous but are out of your control. (Example: "I absolutely *hate* waking up so early every morning for school.")

1. _____

   _____

2. _____

   _____

3. _____

_____

4. _____

_____

5. _____

_____

Now that you've identified some of the things that cause you to waste your time and energy, select one from each section and write down how you might make peace with these situations or use your energy differently when they come up again.

Past

Example: "My father may have left me, but I can't allow his poor choices to keep me down. It's his loss, anyway. In the meantime, I need to be strong for myself, my mom, and my sisters."

_____

_____

_____

_____

Future

Example: "Thinking about college is scary, but it's still a couple years away. Worrying about it now won't do me any good. Instead, I'm going to live in the moment and enjoy my last two years of high school. Besides, just because I won't be living at home doesn't mean my support system is gone. My parents and friends are just a call away anytime I need them."

_____

_____

_____

_____

_____

Out of Your Control

Example: "Yes, waking up at 6 a.m. sucks, but there's really nothing I can do about it, and it's not the end of the world. From now on, I'll just go to bed a little earlier so I won't feel so tired in the morning."

_____

_____

_____

_____

_____

2 Negative to Positive Self-Talk

Close your eyes, and imagine anything in the world *except* a large purple elephant dancing in the streets. Impossible, right? Once I called your attention to it, you *had* to think about it. Negative thinking is the same way. When you tell yourself not to dwell on something negative, you're actually already dwelling on it. Instead of constantly trying to talk yourself *out* of negative thinking, simply start thinking more positively to begin with. This new way of thinking takes a little time and practice (just as any new habit does), but this exercise should help get you started.

On the following lines, write down all of the negative ways you think about stressful situations. Then, rewrite those energy-draining and time-wasting negatives as energy-producing, results-driven positives. Going forward, allow your thoughts to dwell on the new positives, not the old negatives. You'll find yourself feeling better and getting more done in no time. Check out the examples, then do the rest on your own.

Negative: "Don't miss these free throws like you did last game."

Positive: "You got this, man. You've been hitting them all week in practice."

Negative: "My boyfriend's probably cheating on me. He hasn't texted me back in three hours."

Positive: "He's probably really busy studying for his exam. He'll text me back when he's finished."

1. Negative _____

    _____

    _____

Positive _____

_____

_____

2. Negative _____

_____

_____

Positive _____

_____

_____

3. Negative _____

_____

_____

Positive _____

_____

_____

3 What to do with All this Time and Energy?

Finally, now that you've identified all the things that used to keep you wishing, worrying, and whining, and you've shifted your negative self-talk to positive, write down all the new ways you plan to spend your time and emotional energy. In other words, what kinds of things have you been putting off or unable to get around to because you've been so caught up in your negative feelings? Try to come up with as many new areas of focus as you can.

Example: "Now that I'm done stressing about my dad, I'm going to spend more time hanging out with my mom and my sisters."

Example: "Now that I'm no longer worrying about college, I'm going to spend more time focusing on my homework and hanging out with my besties."

Example: "Now that I don't feel so tired in the mornings, I'm going to work really hard to bring up my grades in first period."

1. _____

_____

2. _____

_____

3. _____

_____

4. _____

_____

5. _____

_____

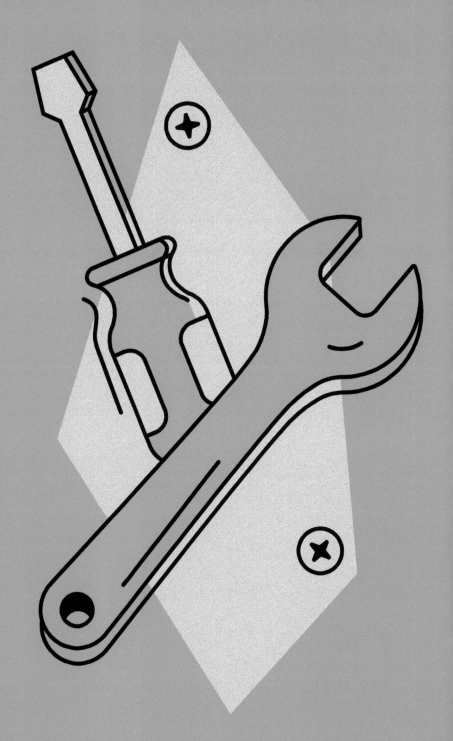

TRUTH N° 7

Healthy Relationships Depend on Self-Empowerment, Not on Trying to Fix Others

Imagine your best friend since kindergarten had recently developed a serious and life-threatening drug addiction, that your brother was thinking of joining a dangerous street gang, or that your mother kept going back to that awful boyfriend who keeps beating her up. How would you respond? I'd be willing to bet that almost instinctively you would probably do whatever it takes to help a loved one to change—especially if what that person is doing is causing them great harm. On the surface, this is a noble goal. Undoubtedly, the world would be a much better place if we were all willing to help a friend—or a stranger— in need. Unfortunately, despite your best efforts, some- times the people you love continue to do things that harm them—and your relationships.

So let's think about your approaches. Would frequent lectures or constant pestering about the dangers of drug addiction *really* stop your friend from getting high? Would a threat to tell your parents about your brother *really* stop him from joining the gang? Do you think giving your mom the silent treatment or insulting her for being "weak" every time she ends up with a black eye would be the thing that *finally* convinces her to leave?

Or maybe you've tried a different tactic. Maybe every time your best friend gets sick from the drugs, you're by her side to take care of her, holding back her hair as she pukes in the toilet, and giving her rides when she's too messed up to drive. Maybe you've tried giving your brother all the money in your savings account just so he wouldn't go out robbing and stealing with his friends. Or maybe you've made a bunch of excuses for your mom every time she gets beat up, like calling her boss to say she's too sick to come to work and doing all the house chores because she's too hurt to move.

Intellectually—or maybe based on experience—you probably already know that none of these tactics work and that it is virtually impossible to force someone to change who isn't ready or doesn't want to change. Yet time and again you find yourself begging, lecturing, threatening, nagging, pleading, scaring, insulting, and punishing people, hoping they will change, but knowing deep down it won't work.

Or maybe you find yourself hoping that the value of your love and friendship will finally be enough to open their eyes to the reality you've been trying for so long to show them. But you know that all of this emotional exhaustion you put yourself through won't do a darn thing. Deep down, you know that they won't change until they're ready to change—or, as people in recovery say, until they hit rock bottom.

Since you already know all of this, the real question you need to ask yourself, then, isn't, "Why won't so-and-so change?"; it's, "Why do I keep investing so much of my emotional energy into trying to change someone who isn't ready to change themselves?"

Temporary Power Over Others Seems Better Than No Power at All

The first and most obvious response to the previous question is that you love the person you are concerned about and don't want to see them harmed or worse. But there is another reason you keep banging your head against that wall: You feel helpless and powerless, and temporary power seems better than no power at all. What I mean is that, despite what you already know—that people don't change until they're ready to—sometimes people *do* change when you beg, plead, threaten, scare, or lecture them. But there are three problems here:

1. These Changes Are Only Temporary

2. They Don't Address the Root Causes of the Problems

3. They May Actually Sometimes Make Things Worse

Let's say we're talking about your friend with the drug addiction. Maybe a little while back she had a really bad scare. Let's say she took too many drugs and was messed up for the whole night—really messed up. Maybe the following day you gave her a hard time, told her all the stupid things she was doing and saying while she was high, lectured her about the dangers of addiction, and threatened to stop being her friend if she continues to use. If your friend has any sense at all, there's a pretty good chance she took what you said to heart and cleaned up her act. Maybe she promised to stop getting high and to get help.

It worked, you might have thought, *I finally got through to her*. And for a short time you both felt good—she was sober, and you were empowered knowing you could control her behavior.

But then something triggered her again—maybe it's her severe anxiety or her abusive relationship with her stepfather. And she's an addict, so she turned to the only thing she knows to ease her pain. But you're her friend, of course, and she didn't want to let you down. So instead of admitting she'd begun using drugs again, she ignored your calls and sort of disappeared for a while—back with those other friends she uses with. But this time her drug use got worse, because on top of using to cope with just her original pain, she's using even more to cover up the guilt and the shame she feels from lying to you, breaking her promises, and ignoring your calls. And so the cycle continues.

As you can see, your tactics might have worked for a short time—your friend may have stopped using for a day or a week or even much longer—but in the end she still has some serious problems she needs to contend with, and nothing has come of your tactics except that she feels even more alienated from you. The truth of the matter is this: You can no more convince your friend—or your brother, your mom, or whomever—to change than you can convince her to grow wings and fly. She has to *want* to change.

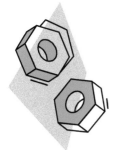

My goal here is not to discourage you or to make you feel that people will never change. If you have friends or loved ones in need, you should continue to love them and to treat them with dignity and respect. But you must also understand that sometimes— most times, actually—you are powerless over others, and that meaningful relationships do not depend on fixing others or making their problems go away for them. Instead of focusing so much of your efforts and energy on the problems of others— even those you love dearly—it may be helpful to focus on the one thing you can change: yourself. After all, you didn't cause their problems, and you can't cure them, but you can learn to cope effectively with how their problems impact you.

Admitting you are powerless over others doesn't mean you are powerless over yourself. Social Black Belt Truth N°7 is that *self*-empowerment—not trying to fix others—is the key to healthy relationships. If you focus on this truth and work to empower *yourself*, you will be able to navigate your difficult relationships from a position of strength, not of weakness. And when your friends and loved ones see the person they love (you!) acting so strong and resilient and empowered—instead of nagging, lecturing, or begging—they're much more likely to want to do the same for themselves.

TIP N°7

POWER UP!

I recognize that Truth N°7 may seem a bit counterintuitive since your instinct is to try to save someone when they're drowning—especially when you care about them—but how can you save someone from drowning when you can hardly swim yourself? Since you've already determined that your previous efforts to change people aren't going to work until your loved ones are ready to change themselves, you have to work on empowering yourself in the meantime. Fortunately, there is a four-step method to help you do this. When you follow these steps and first improve yourself, you'll find that the other person will likely be much more responsive to your needs in the relationship, more aware of his or her own issues, and more motivated to change in a positive way. Let's take a look.

1. Express Your Feelings Appropriately

When speaking to another person about the impacts of their behaviors, it is important to express your feelings using "I" statements instead of "You" statements. For example, instead of telling your friend, "You lied to me when you said you would get help," try saying something like, "I feel really hurt when you say you're going to get help and then don't." Instead of telling your brother, "You're going to end up in prison if you keep riding around with those losers," tell him, "I feel really worried every time you go out with your friends. I love you and don't want to lose you." Expressing your feelings appropriately—rather than criticizing or putting your loved ones down—empowers you by allowing you to take ownership of your feelings, and it frees you from the burden of trying to change others who aren't ready to change. Plus, if you approach your loved ones with respect and concern, rather than with attacks or accusations, they are much less likely to be defensive and much more likely to be open to what you have to say.

2. Make a Specific Request

Instead of issuing threats or demands of your loved ones, try using your power to make a specific request. For example, instead of threatening your mom with, "If you don't leave your boyfriend immediately, I'm moving in with my dad," try something like, "Mom, I love you, and I'm worried about you. I see that you're going through a hard time with your relationship, but I don't feel safe here. If you decide to stay with your boyfriend, that is your decision, but I would like to live with my father until something changes." By linking your request to move out with your feeling of being unsafe, you are clearly identifying that your mother's decision to stay is affecting you in a negative way, and that changing her behavior will improve the situation. You are not judging, and you are not telling your mom what she should do. You are simply stating how you feel and requesting a specific action that will make you feel better.

---

3. Set Boundaries for Yourself and Enforce Them

Staying empowered in healthy relationships means marking off your turf in well-defined and reasonable ways and defending it when necessary. Businesses do it all the time so their customers don't take advantage of them. For example, your cell phone provider charges a small late fee when you pay your bill late. Similarly, when you get caught speeding, the government charges you a fine. I'm sure you can imagine what would happen if these boundaries—and the penalties for violating them—were not well established or weren't enforced.

Just like companies establish and enforce boundaries, you can do the same in your personal relationships. For example, telling your best friend that she's not allowed to tag you in negative posts on social media is a well-defined and reasonable boundary. Telling your boyfriend he is not allowed to curse at you when he's angry is another.

But boundaries, like vampires and good combs, need teeth. Otherwise, you're just flapping your gums. Setting boundaries without enforcing them is like putting a sign up on your front gate that says, "Do not enter!... unless you want to...and if you do, I won't say anything about it." That's lamer than a lemur without a femur! If you want people you have relationships with to respect your boundaries, you have to be willing to enforce them. If your friend keeps getting you caught up in drama because she tags you in negative posts after you've already warned her about it, unfollow her. If your boyfriend keeps cursing angrily at you after you've warned him about it, find another one or be single.

As we discussed in chapter 5, when you make it clear to others what you will and will not permit them to do to you—and what the consequences of violating those boundaries will be—you maintain a position of self-empowerment and ensure that others will treat you the way you want and deserve to be treated. If you don't want others to walk all over you (or your yard), tell them you won't allow it—and mean it!

4. Take Proper Care of Yourself

I know what you're thinking: *Duh, Dr. Cortman. Obviously I should take proper care of myself.* But this is easier said than done, and unfortunately many people simply don't do it when it comes to their personal relationships. The bottom line is this: If you don't take care of yourself, you'll find yourself in unhealthy situations with others who won't respect you or your boundaries. While you can't—and shouldn't—always take care of other people, you can always take care of yourself. And when you take care of yourself, you simultaneously show others how you expect them to treat you.

Let's say you have a new car that you expect others to respect and keep clean when you're kind enough to give them rides to school. If you take care of the car, others will see that and will likely do the same. But if you tell others you expect them to respect your car while you're trashing it up right in front of them, then it's unreasonable to expect much better from them. Now here's the deal: You don't have to give anyone a ride. If you have a new car that you're clearly taking care of, and you tell your friends you expect them to do the same and they don't— well, it sounds to me like they need to catch the bus tomorrow morning. If you set an example of self-care and self-respect, your friends and loved ones will follow your lead. If you don't, they will follow that lead too. If you want others to respect you, then you need to show them how it's done.

Being Weak When You Need to be Strong

Here's the problem with enabling others who take advantage of you and won't take care of themselves: While you think you're being *strong* by propping *them* up all the time, you're actually being *weak* by not standing up for *yourself.* And when you constantly give and give to others who only take and take, eventually you'll have nothing left for yourself. Not only that, but when you constantly help others who won't help themselves, you actually weaken them, too, by not allowing them to be strong enough to get better on their own.

Now let me be clear: In no way am I suggesting you should not help others in need. Caring for others and helping them when they are down is what good people do. But this kind of generosity is not what I'm talking about. What I'm referring to in this chapter, and what Truth N°7 is all about, is not allowing others to endlessly drain all of the good out of you while never giving back and never doing anything for themselves. When you give someone all your power, you have none left for yourself, and this is no way to live your life. Good relationships— real, healthy, *positive* relationships—are mutually beneficial. In other words, they are good for both parties, not just one.

Helping vs. Enabling

So how do you know the difference between helping a friend in need and enabling someone to continue with situations that are harmful to both of you? Here are a couple of ways to help you think about this dilemma: If you're helping someone who is trying to help themselves but for some reason still needs a hand, then by all means, help a friend in need. But if you are doing something for someone that they can do for themselves and won't, you are probably enabling. If you're working harder to solve problems in someone else's life than they are, you are enabling.

For example, if your best friend asks you to help her clean her room, and you are both having a good time and sharing in the work, then you're just helping a friend—a completely fine thing to do. But, if you do all the work while she sits on her phone and bosses you around, you're enabling. If you give your friend rides to her counseling sessions to treat her addiction, you're helping. If you drive her around while she gets high, you're definitely enabling. Or, if your brother is failing chemistry class and you tutor him or help him with his homework, you're helping. If you *do* his homework while he's nowhere to be found, well, you get the point.

Maybe this is a better way to look at it: If what you're doing makes you feel *good,* you're probably helping. If what you're doing makes you feel *used,* then you're probably enabling. Helpers feel proud of their behavior; enablers feel ashamed. Helpers feel strong; enablers feel weak. Helpers feel appreciated; enablers feel resentful. Sometimes it pays to go with your gut. Next time you're in a situation with a friend or a loved one, monitor how you feel. If something feels right, then it probably is. If something feels wrong, that's probably the case as well.

Here's the bottom line of Truth N°7: You should be willing to help others, but you cannot change other people who aren't ready or willing to change themselves. Further, you should not allow others to take advantage of you or drag you down with them. Instead of enabling others, find strength in empowering yourself. Any change that takes place within a relationship must start with *you.* You can't help others until you are in a good place, so be willing to put in the hard work to evolve in a positive direction, and others around you will do the same. These simple rules are the keys to maintaining and strengthening healthy relationships while avoiding the pitfalls of being taken advantage of. As we've already discussed, sometimes change is really hard. Sometimes standing up to loved ones takes a lot of courage. That's why so many people stay stuck in the ruts of bad relationships—they're either afraid to change or don't know how. But you are strong, and you can do it. Below are some exercises to help you be empowered.

———

EXERCISES

———

Though it may be hard to realize that your best efforts to help people are sometimes in vain, the following exercises can help you re-apply those good intentions where they will be best served: on your own self-empowerment. Here, you're going to identify those you've tried to change and all the ways you've struck out. Then, after learning to express your feelings appropriately, you'll begin to set new boundaries and assert yourself appropriately.

Identify the Problem Relationship

Think of the person in your life who you're most often frustrated with and whose harmful behavior you tend to enable. Is it your boyfriend and his constant cheating? Your mom and her dangerous drinking? Or maybe it's your best friend and her constant disrespect of you in front of others? Write a few sentences below describing the person and behavior that has been hurting you for so long.

_____

_____

_____

_____

_____

_____

_____

_____

_____

_____

_____

_____

_____

② Assess Your Enabling Tendencies

Now that you've identified the person and behavior that hurts you the most, you need to take an honest look at all the unproductive ways you have tried to get this person to change. Below are some of the most common tactics people use (unsuccessfully) to try to get others to change. For each one, describe what you did or said when using this tactic as well as how the person acted in response.

TACTIC	WHAT YOU DID OR SAID	HOW THE OTHER PERSON RESPONDED
SARCASM/ RUDENESS		
GUILT TRIPS		
SHOUTING/ SCREAMING		
THREATS		
AVOIDANCE/ SILENT TREATMENT		

3 Practice Expressing Your Feelings

Now that you've identified which tactics haven't worked, you need to practice what *will* work. For this exercise, instead of using "You" statements and forcing others to become defensive, practice communicating your feelings directly using "I" statements. For example, instead of saying, "You're an untrustworthy liar," say, "I find it hard to trust you when you tell me things that aren't true." Using the examples from exercise 2, write a few non-accusatory "I" statements to let that person know how their behavior impacts you.

1. I _____

   _____ ,

   when you _____

   _____ .

2. I _____

   _____ ,

   when you _____

   _____ .

3. I _____

   _____ ,

   when you _____

   _____ .

4 Identify Your Boundaries...
and the Consequences for Crossing Them

If your boyfriend, girlfriend, best friend, sibling or whoever chooses to continue in unhealthy and unacceptable behaviors that violate the boundaries you've set, you need to have options ready to enforce them. In this exercise, describe the boundary-crossing behavior and three enforcement actions you will be willing to take if it happens again.

IF...	I WILL...
Karen disrespects me in front of other people again,	1. stop giving her rides to school, 2. unfollow her on social media, 3. and not speak to her again until she apologizes to me publicly and promises not to do it again.
	1. 2. 3.
	1. 2. 3.
	1. 2. 3.

⑤ ASSERT Yourself

Now that you've identified the problem person and behavior and the tactics that don't work, created a few go-to "I" statements, and set boundaries and consequences, it's time to really empower yourself! Next time your boundaries are crossed, ASSERT yourself by following this simple formula.

A: Gain the **attention** of the other person.
S: Do this **soon** after the problem behavior occurs.
S: Be **specific** about the behavior without attacking the other person.
E: Use "I" statements to describe the **effect** their behavior has on you.
R: Describe what kind of **response** (new behavior) you expect from this person.
T: Describe the new **terms** of the relationship and how it will be impacted if they violate them.

Next, apply the ASSERT formula to a relationship in your life. Write what you will do and say at each step.

A: How will you gain the **attention** of the other person?

_____

_____

_____

_____

_____

S: How **soon** after the incident will you have this discussion? Right away?
A few days later, after things have cooled down?

_____

_____

_____

_____

_____

S: What **specific** behavior will you talk about?

_____

_____

_____

_____

_____

E: What **effects** of this behavior will you describe using "I" statements?

_____

_____

_____

_____

_____

R: What kind of **response** (new behavior) do you expect from this person?

_____

_____

_____

_____

T: What new **terms** of the relationship will you put into effect
if the new response is violated?

_____

_____

_____

_____

TRUTH N° 8

Ego Boundaries Protect Us from Rejection, Insult, and Intimidation

Have you ever received a gift, maybe for a birthday or a holiday, that you didn't really want but were forced by your parents to keep? When I was a kid, my aunt always gave me and my siblings jigsaw puzzles for our birthdays, despite the fact that we had never once indicated that we enjoyed putting them together. So every year my mom would force us to lie on the floor, put some of the puzzle together, and pretend to be lost in the joy of puzzling so she could take an "impromptu" photo of us eagerly playing with the gift. After the photo was taken and sent to my aunt, the puzzle was broken down, reboxed, and placed in its new home—the dark recesses of my bed-room closet—where it would stay until the next spring cleaning, when it would be packed up with all the other junk we never played with and sent off to Goodwill. Like-wise, my grandmother—that sweet angel of a woman—never failed to give me an ugly sweater for Christmas. Not an ugly *Christmas* sweater, mind you—just a *regular* ugly one. And as she did with the puzzles from my aunt, my mother forced me to keep these awful fashion disasters in my closet so that I could "just happen to be wearing them" the next time my grandmother came to visit a few weeks or months later. Ugh, the agony of receiving gifts! On the outside I had to pretend I was ecstatic and surprised every time I opened them, but on the inside I screamed "Death to sweaters and puzzles! May they all burn in Hell!"

Despite what most of us are taught about how to receive gifts—appreciate that you were thought of at all, express gratitude, and never, *ever* regift *back to the same person who gave it to you the year before*—the truth of the matter is that probably most of us would prefer to be more honest about how we feel about them. If I had told my grandmother when I was 10 that I didn't like the sweaters she gave me and didn't want any more—even though I genuinely appreciated her kindness and generosity— perhaps I wouldn't still be receiving them every year at Christmas and going through the routine of exchanging them at the store for something a little more my style. Of course, puzzles and ugly sweaters are relatively harmless gifts, but what if you're on the receiving end of something much more serious, like racism, sexism, homophobia, anger, jealousy, insecurity, or the like? Being able to reject these "gifts," then, is much more important than rejecting puzzles, but does that mean it is also much more difficult? The Buddha says no.

Among the many stories about the Buddha is one in which he was in a small village surrounded by supporters of his message. But one man in particular was not a fan, and he raged at the Buddha, accusing him of being a liar and a thief. The Buddha let the man finish yelling and then kindly asked him, "If someone gives you a gift, and you reject it, to whom does the gift belong?" The man responded rudely, "It still belongs to the person giving it, obviously." Calmly, the Buddha responded, "You are correct. You may keep your anger for yourself, because we reject it." In this chapter, you will see how and why it is important to establish boundaries between yourself and others so that you do not take on and internalize their negative traits. First I will tell you Marta's story. Then I will explain how you, too, can create a crucially important space between the awesomeness of yourself and the occasional negativity of others.

Marta is 16 and lives in a small, working-class town in the Midwest where most of the residents are white, but many of the residents are Mexican- and Central American-natives who work seasonally on the local farms. Last week Marta saw a sign in the window of one of the local diners that said, "Hiring Servers, Bi-lingual a Plus," and decided to apply. Even though it was her first job interview and she was really nervous, Marta gave excellent answers to all the manager's questions. About 20 minutes into the interview, though, the diner got so busy that Doug, the manager, had to break away from Marta's interview to help with some of the tables. Always quick on her feet and never one to slack while others around her work hard, Marta jumped up from where she was sitting and walked around the diner offering to refill customers' drinks and helping to clear dirty tables. She greeted customers as they came in and held the door for them as they left, thanking them for stopping in and reminding them to "Come again soon." At one point, Marta even stepped in to translate part of the menu for a table of young migrant workers who were struggling to read English. Doug was so impressed by Marta's work ethic and positive attitude that when things finally slowed down, he didn't even ask Marta to finish the interview—he just hired her on the spot!

Even though work as a server is notoriously difficult, Marta's first two shifts at the diner were awesome. She learned the server lingo and became friendly with the cooks. She studied the moves of a veteran server and learned to balance heavy trays filled with dirty dishes. She greeted every customer with a hearty "Hello" and a big smile as they came in, waited on customers in both English and Spanish, and told them with all sincerity that she couldn't wait to see them again. All of the customers were really nice to Marta and patient when they realized she was new, and for her hard work and upbeat attitude, most of them left generous tips—even the poor migrant workers who probably didn't have much to spare.

During her third shift, however, Marta experienced her first difficult customers. It was during the dinner rush when lots of the farm workers come in after their long, hard days and when Marta finds herself doing a lot of translating from the menu that an older couple came in and rudely asked for a table. Marta courteously showed them to their table and politely asked what she could get them to drink. "Water," they replied curtly. When Marta returned with their drinks, it was more of the same. "I'll have the steak," the man said, "Medium rare." "Give me the chicken," said his wife, "and don't overcook it." And the rest of the meal was the same. No "please," no "Thank you." They never smiled and never made eye contact. Marta wasn't sure what she had done to upset them, but she gave them excellent, fast customer service, nonetheless. And when they were finished, she walked them to the door and sincerely invited them to "Come again soon."

After the couple left, Marta scooped up their check and the small bills and loose coins they had left and quickly cleared the table to make room for the next customers. When she went back to the counter to ring up the sale, however, Marta couldn't believe what she saw. For the check of $26.52, they left exact change—$26.52—and on the line that says tip, they wrote, in large, aggressive scrawl, "Go back to Mexico! We don't tip illegals."

Marta was shocked, confused, and really, really insulted. She had heard stories like this from her mother and from some of her father's friends who worked on the farms, but Marta had never experienced such blatant and cruel racism firsthand. *Why would someone do this,* she asked herself. For starters, she was an American, born and raised right there in her small town, and so were her parents and grandparents. But beyond that, she wondered, *Why does it matter where I'm from?* Marta didn't care if those white customers were from America, Canada, Whitelandia, or Mars—she had simply always treated everyone with the utmost courtesy and respect and had come to expect the same from them in return. How anyone could treat another person—a child, no less—so cruelly was beyond Marta's comprehension. And while she was genuinely hurt by their insult—and even spent a few minutes crying in the bathroom—Marta ultimately found herself just feeling *sorry* for those mean people and wondering what terrible things had happened in their lives that had made them so prejudiced and cruel.

After taking a few minutes for herself, Marta dried her eyes and headed back out to finish her shift with the same bright smile she had started it with. And when she was done, Marta put in her earbuds, hopped on her bike, and blasted her favorite song, singing loudly and shaking off the haters with every hard push of the pedals.

If you're like most people, right now you're probably thinking of all the ways you would have responded to Marta's situation, and I'm guessing most of them are nothing like Marta's. The question, then, is *How do we protect ourselves from the mean and hurtful words and actions of others?* And the answer is ego boundaries.

Drawing a Line Between Yourself and Others

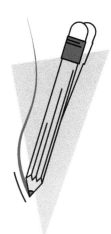

A boundary is a line that separates something from something else, and the word *ego* is a Latin word that means "I," so an ego boundary is simply an awareness of where you end and where another person begins. Everything you do, say, or think is a statement about you, and everything *I* do, say, or think is a statement about me. So if I treat you badly, this says a whole lot about me and almost nothing about you. If I am kind to you, this does not make *you* a kind person; it makes *me* one. Likewise, if I disrespect you or treat you rudely, this does not indicate you are unworthy of respect; it indicates that I sometimes treat people with disrespect and rudeness. So the sooner you recognize that other people's words and actions—

their anger, their prejudice, their jealousy—are statements about them and not about you, the sooner you, like Marta, will be able to shake off their bad behavior and go about your merry way.

There is a term in psychology called *projection.* Projection occurs when people attach their own traits onto other people, and projection can be sometimes positive and sometimes negative. An example: People who cheat in relationships often accuse their partners of cheating, even when there is no evidence that they are. Likewise, thieves often suspect others of plotting to steal from them, and liars often suspect others are lying, even when none of this is the case. Conversely, people who are faithful and honest generally expect the same from others and only suspect them of misdeeds if they have good reason to.

It's important to keep projection in mind when interacting with other people so you won't be constantly vulnerable to their comments or actions. If your best friend makes a rude comment about your weight, it's not because you're undeserving of respect; it's because she—at least in that moment—has forgotten how to treat others with kindness. It may also be a sign that she feels insecure about her *own* looks, and she thinks putting others down will make her feel better. In other words, it's not *your* problem that she's rude or insecure, it's hers. Now, don't get me wrong, I know words can hurt, and we are all sometimes impacted by the behaviors of others, but creating ego boundaries is a great way to lessen their blow.

You Are Not Responsible for What Others Say and Do

Recall this rhyme from when you were a little kid: "I am rubber, and you are glue. Whatever you say bounces off me and sticks to you." Marta is rubber, and you can be, too. But many people struggle to be rubber-like. Instead, they allow their feelings of self-worth to be determined by the way others treat them. In other words, they aren't good at setting ego boundaries. When people mistreat them, they often find themselves asking, *What's wrong with me?* instead of *Why was that other person so hurtful?* In my decades of psychotherapy, I have seen countless people who have been the victims of others' misdeeds who believe that the reason they were cheated on, sexually abused, insulted, or abandoned is that they were *unworthy* of love, respect, or companionship. And in almost every single case, this was simply not true.

My young friend Jada was 16 when her school counselor referred her to my practice. For several years, Jada's teachers had noted that she exhibited signs of depression, and she had recently been caught using drugs at school. After a couple difficult sessions of counseling, Jada revealed to me a painful secret—for 10 years she had been sexually abused by her father, who had died just a few months before. Understandably, the decade of physical and psychological abuse took a serious toll on Jada's mental health. She felt betrayed by her family and ashamed of her abuse and, as a result, came to view herself as used, dirty, and unlovable. In the end, Jada's trauma found relief in the form of marijuana and pills.

In therapy, Jada frequently asked me *what she had done* to deserve such treatment. So, in addition to working with her to kick her addictions, I had to convince Jada that she was the *victim* of these crimes, not the perpetrator, so she should no longer continue to punish herself with depression and drug abuse for wrongs that she never committed. As painful as her experiences were, the behaviors were not hers to own. It took a long time—many sessions over many months—but eventually Jada bounced back. By creating ego boundaries—in other words, by recognizing that the actions of her father were a reflection of *his* shortcomings, not hers—Jada began to see that a lifetime of self-punishment would only make her situation worse, not better. Eventually, Jada let go of the anger and shame of her dark past and began to see herself for what she truly is: a beautiful young woman with a bright future ahead of her.

So What Part *Is* Yours?

Social Black Belt Truth N°8 is all about being comfortable with yourself and not allowing the naysayers to get you down, but this does not mean you should never listen to what others have to say. There's an old saying that people in support groups use to help them deal with criticism: "If it doesn't apply, let it fly." In other words, if what someone says about you—that you're a jerk, a liar, or a really bad singer—simply isn't true, well, who cares? Let it fly. Be the rubber.

But there's another old saying you may want to keep in mind here: "If the shoe fits, wear it." In other words, sometimes you need to consider the possibility that the things others say about you are *true*. Maybe you *are* a jerk, a liar, or a really bad singer. Just because someone else says so doesn't make it untrue. While creating boundaries is important—crucial, even—to maintaining a positive sense of self, this is not an excuse to form barriers against the feedback of others. It's important to understand that creating and maintaining ego boundaries does not give you permission to ignore your own character flaws simply because someone else points them out to you. Sometimes you need to be the glue.

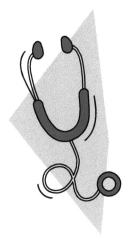

Critical reflection of feedback from others is essential to personal growth. If your boss tells you that you need to do better at work, maybe you do. If your teacher tells you that you need to do better in class, maybe you do. While it's important not to allow your self-worth to be determined by the opinions of others, it's equally important to take what others say into consideration when determining the appropriateness of your behavior. If one person tells you, "You're one sick puppy," they're probably kidding. If two people say it, then it's probably a coincidence. But if *everyone* keeps telling you that you're one sick puppy, well, maybe you need to go to the vet.

So how do you know when to be the rubber and when to be the glue? In other words, how do you know when to let the words and actions bounce off of you and when to let them sink in? One way to keep these boundaries in place is to think of your life as a movie in which you're the star (of course), and the people in your life play supporting roles. In movies, there are types—the good guy, the bad guy, the bully, the geek, and so on—and while sometimes the good guy turns bad or the geek becomes sexy, in most cases these characters remain true to their type. Well, life typically works the same way. That kid who's been stealing people's lunch money since first grade doesn't suddenly decide to start a fundraiser for the local soup kitchen any more than the social butterfly suddenly becomes shy. Just like in the movies, these sudden 180s generally don't ring true.

Your close friends and family are the same way, and understanding their "type" might help you evaluate the significance of their comments and behavior toward you. For example, if your goofy cousin Vincent has been calling you silly names since you were kids and greets you with, "What up, duckface," that doesn't mean you can fly. That's just Vincent being Vincent. But if your sweet Aunt Irma has always been truthful and honest with you and expresses genuine concern about changes she's noticed in your behavior lately, maybe you should hear what she has to say. Creating boundaries to keep negativity out only works if you are also willing to sometimes let positivity in. In both cases, the result of these boundaries is a better and more secure you.

———

ESTABLISH AND DEFEND YOUR BOUNDARIES

Maintaining ego boundaries by knowing where you end and where others begin will protect you from the potential threats of your interactions with them. By defending your boundaries, you will know how to react when others insult, degrade, or otherwise disrespect you. And trust me, they will. It doesn't matter how good you are to others, some-times people just aren't very nice. And sometimes, if the person is someone close to you, they will hit you where it hurts the most. But by working to establish and maintain your ego boundaries, you will be better equipped to deflect their emotional blows.

Ultimately, it doesn't matter who the insulter is—your best friend, your mom, or some random person at the grocery store. What matters is that, like Marta, you recognize that their insults or inconsiderate acts are about them, not you. And when you stop taking every negative interaction so personally, you will no longer feel as devastated by people's actions as you were before. And here is the best part: When this happens, you will be able to do things you might have avoided before, like going to parties, speaking in public, or talking to new people, because you will no longer be afraid that every interaction has to go perfectly and because you will no longer feel so affected by others' reactions.

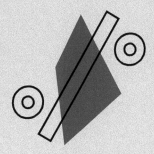

Remember, defining and maintaining your ego boundaries means not worrying so much about what others think or how they act toward you. You are not responsible for their thoughts, feelings, or actions. You are only responsible for your own. People will do what they do and say what they say. That won't change. What *must* change, however, is how you allow them to make you feel. People's mean words and actions will only hurt you if you let them.

If you want people to treat you well, show them how it's done. Lead by example and be nice to them first. Always strive to be your best self, and be willing to put yourself out there a little without always living in fear of what others might think. Finally, don't be afraid to be honest with yourself. Be open to learning more about yourself through others whose advice you respect, and be willing to make positive changes as often as possible. When you do this, no one will be able to knock you down.

EXERCISES

———

Truth N°8 is all about drawing an emotional boundary between you and others to protect yourself from their occasional mean words and actions while at the same time knowing who you can trust to offer constructive criticism worth paying attention to. The following exercises will give you some strategies to begin that process.

① Create Your Ego Boundaries

The goal of this exercise is to help you get used to separating your values and beliefs from those of other people—in other words, to begin creating your ego boundaries. Start by thinking of some key people in your life and topics that sometimes create tension or problems in those relationships. For instance, maybe you and your parents don't see eye-to-eye on religious matters or what you plan to do after high school, or maybe you and your brother don't have the same warm feelings about his new girlfriend. Whatever people and topics you choose, first think about the ways you see things in common; then think carefully about the ways you see things differently. Finally, write a few words about what it means that you don't agree. Follow the example below to help you get started.

PERSON/ SITUATION	"My younger brother has a new girlfriend who has a reputation for drinking and using drugs and messing around with different guys at parties."
WHERE WE AGREE	"My brother and I agree that he's old enough to have a girlfriend and that he has as much a right to be happy as I do. We also agree that his girlfriend is very sweet to him when they're together."
WHERE WE DISAGREE	"My brother thinks his new girlfriend can do no wrong and that what other people say about her are only rumors, but I have seen her wasted at two parties making out with random guys. Maybe she'll be different now that she's in a relationship, but I just think my brother can do better. I'm also afraid that she'll hurt him by cheating on him or, worse, that she'll influence him to start getting messed up at parties, too."
WHAT IT ALL MEANS	"Ultimately my brother is his own person who has to make his own decisions—good and bad. He may be right about his new girlfriend. Maybe she is a really sweet girl who has just made a few mistakes—I mean, who hasn't?—but I'm his big sister, so I'm allowed to be worried about him. In the end, there's really nothing I can do to stop him. I mean, it's not like I can force them to break up. So in the meantime, I will just try to respect his choices as much as possible and be there for him whenever he needs me."

PERSON/ SITUATION	
WHERE WE AGREE	
WHERE WE DISAGREE	
WHAT IT ALL MEANS	

PERSON/ SITUATION	
WHERE WE AGREE	
WHERE WE DISAGREE	
WHAT IT ALL MEANS	

② Cast Your Movie

Have you always wanted to star in a movie? Well, now you can. For this exercise, pretend your life is a movie and you, of course, are the star. Like any movie, yours must have a supporting cast, so think about the people who figure prominently in your day-to-day life. They can be your parents, your siblings, your friends, or anyone else you spend a lot of time around. The purpose of this activity, however, is not simply to imagine yourself on the big screen—although, on second thought, it never hurts to dream. Your job here is to think about the ways the people around you typically act out their roles so you know what to expect from them and won't be hurt when they play their parts. For each person, think of a few words to describe them, find the perfect word to describe their role, and write a brief plan of how you will handle them next time they behave in character. Use the following examples as a guide.

SUPPORTING ROLE	TYPICAL BEHAVIORS	PERFECT NAME FOR ROLE	HOW I WILL ACT NEXT TIME THEY PLAY THEIR ROLE
Mom	"My mom can be really overprotective sometimes. She's always in my business and always tries to micromanage me. Sometimes she just doesn't know when to let up."	"The Hawk"	"Next time my mom gets in my business, I will try to be more patient with her. I understand that she is acting out of love and that she only wants the best for me. Yes, she can be super annoying, but I'd rather have a mom who looks out too much than one who doesn't look out at all. Plus, it's not really that bad. She's kept me out of trouble a few times, and she's always there when I need someone to talk to."
My Cousin, Steven	"Steven can be really goofy and obnoxious sometimes. He's always cracking jokes about stuff he knows I'm sensitive about. Sometimes he's funny, but a lot of the time he hurts my feelings."	"The Joker"	"Next time Steven cracks jokes on me and hurts my feelings, I'll be more vocal about how I feel. I'll also try not to be so sensitive about some of the things he says since I know he's just kidding and that he really loves me."

SUPPORTING ROLE	TYPICAL BEHAVIORS	PERFECT NAME FOR ROLE	HOW I WILL ACT NEXT TIME THEY PLAY THEIR ROLE

3 Protect Yourself From Those Negative Feelings

For this exercise, think back to three times when other people's actions have made you feel hurt, embarrassed, ashamed, worthless, stupid, or hopeless. First, write an honest assessment of how those interactions made you feel. Then, write how you can protect yourself from hurt feelings next time a similar situation arises. Use the example to get you started.

Example: "When my boyfriend told me I was boring for not wanting to hang out with his friends, I was really hurt. For a long time after that, I thought maybe he was right, so I did all kinds of things he was interested in, even though I didn't really enjoy them. I realize now that I'm not a boring person at all—we just have different interests, and there's nothing wrong with that at all. Next time he says things that hurt my feelings, I will speak up for myself, and I won't let his mean words change how I feel about myself."

1. _____

_____

_____

_____

_____

_____

_____

_____

_____

_____

2. _____

_____

_____

_____

_____

_____

_____

_____

_____

_____

_____

3. _____

_____

_____

_____

_____

_____

_____

_____

_____

_____

_____

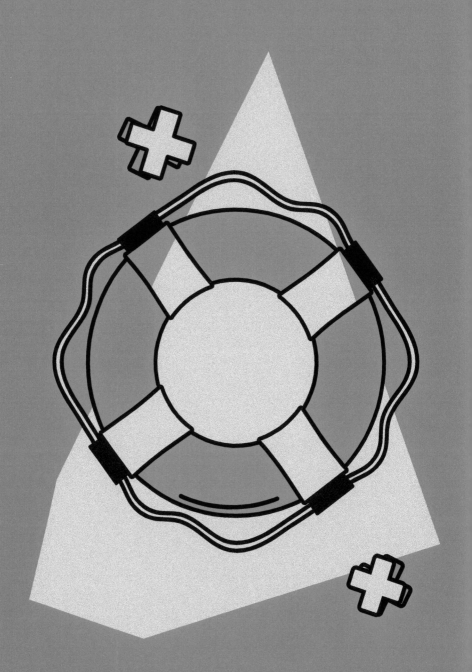

TRUTH N° 9

You Can Trust People to be Who They Are, Not Who You Want Them to Be

Erica was 17 and just starting her junior year when her parents brought her to me to help her work through her depression. Through lots of tears, Erica told me about the recent breakup of her relationship with Carter, a boy she had been dating since the summer before their sophomore year, when they were both 15. The night Erica met Carter at her best friend Taylor's birthday party, Carter was already dating Stefani, another close friend of Erica's. Erica knew Stefani had been dating some really cute boy on the lacrosse team—that was *all* Stefani had been talking about for the prior three weeks, after all—but she didn't realize just *how* cute Carter was until he showed up that night holding Stefani's hand. When Erica saw Carter, she was immediately attracted to him—and seriously jealous of Stefani.

Throughout the evening, Erica couldn't help looking over at Carter every chance she got, and—well, maybe it was just in her head—but she swore she saw Carter checking her out, too. Around midnight, Stefani's mom picked

her up, but Carter told Stefani he wanted to stay a little longer at the party and that he'd catch a ride home with Trevor, his best friend from the lacrosse team. As the late night turned into early morning, a few other people left the party, and eventually there were just four people remaining—Taylor and Erica, Carter and Trevor.

Taylor and Trevor chatted nervously for a little while, but mostly they sat on opposite ends of the couch—popcorn bowl between them—and watched a goofy movie in awkward silence. It was pretty obvious that there was no attraction between them and that nothing was going to happen. Meanwhile, Erica and Carter sat together on the loveseat across from Taylor and Trevor—*no* popcorn between them—and slowly inched closer and closer until, before she even realized what had happened, Erica was cuddled up snugly inside Carter's arms and chest. When the movie ended, Taylor went to bed and Trevor headed home. But Erica and Carter hardly noticed they were gone—because they had been making out so hard no one could get their attention.

At the start of Taylor's birthday party the evening before, Erica had never even met Carter—although she *had* heard whispers about his reputation—and Carter was dating Erica's friend Stefani. Now, just a few hours later, things were very different. At six in the morning, just as the sun was starting to reveal itself to what should have been another ordinary day, Carter whispered in Erica's ear how much he cared about her, how he knew at first sight that he just *had* to be with her, and that he and Stefani were really just friends, anyway. Believing every word Carter said, Erica betrayed her close friend and gave away her virginity to a really cute guy from the lacrosse team whom she hardly knew at all.

As you might expect, Erica fell instantly in love with Carter. Her relationship with Stefani and her reputation at school were totally destroyed, but none of that mattered to Erica. She had Carter, and everyone else was just jealous, she thought. At first their relationship was really great. True, many people talked a lot of trash about Carter cheating on Stefani and about Erica stealing her friend's boyfriend, but neither of them cared what other people said. If anything, the drama they went through together made them even closer. They were in love, and they were in this together, so forget everyone else.

Stefani never forgave Erica, but eventually most of her other friends did. And Carter's friends were cool either way—they didn't care who Carter dated or who he cheated on in the slightest. Eventually, as it tends to do, time passed, people stopped talking trash about them, and life got back to normal.

Throughout the first couple months of their relationship, Erica and Carter did what most teenagers in relationships do—they hung out, went to the movies, texted each other all day long, and watched a lot of Netflix. But it didn't take long before Carter started spending a lot more time with his boys and acting a lot shadier toward Erica. Whereas he used to text her back right away, now Carter sometimes took hours to respond to Erica's triple heart emojis—and sometimes he didn't text her back at all. And the next day at school it was always the same excuses. "My phone was dead" or "I was playing lacrosse with Trevor, and I forgot to check my phone."

For a while Erica had no choice but to believe Carter—even if she was a little hurt *and* really annoyed—but then she started hearing rumors that Carter wasn't quite where he said he had been. Erica's friend Jen said she thought she saw Carter at the movies with another girl, but Carter denied it. Then, Santino from second period said he saw Carter at a party dancing with some sophomore, and Carter denied that too. This he-said-she-

said went on for more than a year, with Erica constantly accusing and Carter constantly denying, but eventually the truth came out. One day at lunch, Erica's friend Jen told her she had something to tell her—*and* show her. Jen said she was getting into her car at the mall the day before when she noticed two people making out in the car next to hers. At first, she said, she had just laughed at them and was about to pull out of her parking spot, but then she realized who she was looking at—it was Carter, all over some girl who was definitely *not* Erica. So Jen did what any good friend would do—she pulled out her phone and filmed the whole thing.

When Erica saw the video, her heart dropped into her stomach, and she confronted Carter that day after school. At first he denied he was even at the mall the day before, but when Erica showed him the video, he knew he was caught. Carter confessed that he was the boy in the video, and when Erica asked him about all the other times she had heard rumors about him, he admitted that he had been cheating on Erica for the entire year they had been together. Erica was crushed, heartbroken, devastated.

Erica broke up with Carter on the spot, but she had a really hard time moving on. She felt embarrassed and betrayed. She felt *used.* Over the next few weeks, lots of people at school turned on Erica. Instead of comforting her, they told her she got what she deserved for breaking up Carter and Stefani the year before. Things were even worse on social media. People were brutal.

Eventually Erica stopped going to school, and when she came to my office, she had missed more than two weeks straight. In therapy, she kept asking one question: "How could Carter *do* this to me?! I *trusted* him!" To help Erica find an answer to that question and make sense of her situation, I told her about the scorpion and the frog.

Once upon a time in a land far, far away, there lived a frog named Philip whose greatest pleasure in life was helping unfortunate land-based critters who could not swim very well to cross the dangerous creek where he lived. Day and night, night and day, Philip the Frog sat by the muddy banks waiting for his friends like Timmy the Tick, Ricky the Roach, and Spencer the Spider to come by the creek to be ferried across on his back. But there was one little devil who Philip absolutely refused to help cross because he had a bad reputation for stabbing others in the back—Scotty the Scorpion. For years, Scotty had been begging Philip for a ride, sweet talking him with compliments about how nice his warts looked or bribing him with treats like mosquitoes, flies, and ladybugs, but Philip never gave in.

One day, as he had many times before, Scotty came by the creek and asked Philip for a ride across. He claimed his sweet Aunt Scarletta, who lived on the other side, was old and frail and desperately needed someone to look after her in her final days. Scotty begged and pleaded, cried and cajoled, but still Philip refused. He said, "Scotty, I'm sorry, but I just can't trust you. You have a reputation for stabbing others in the back." Denied yet again, Scotty began to scuttle away, but before he did, he turned to Philip and said, "You know, Philip, I'm not as bad as they say I am, and if I wanted to sting you, I would have done it by now. Besides, what good would it do me to stab you in the back? I mean, if I were to stab you and you began to drown, wouldn't I just be drowning myself in the process? Well, I guess I'll be on my way now. I promise I won't bother you again, Philip."

As Scotty turned again to leave, Philip called after him, "Wait, Scotty, you're right. You've never done me wrong, and you've had plenty of opportunities to stab me in the back and you never did. And what you say makes perfect sense. You're not a strong swimmer, and you need me to help you cross. If I go down, you go down, and I just don't see that happening. I'm sorry I doubted you, buddy. Hop on. I'd be glad to take you to see your sweet Aunt Scarletta."

And with that, they were off. Scotty the Scorpion clung tightly to the back of Philip the Frog as they made their way gently across the wide, slow-moving creek. Along the way they had a nice conversation and got to know each other a little better. It turns out the two frenemies had a lot in common— their love of certain delicious bugs, for example. They even lived in the same neighborhood, near the rusty old bicycle half-buried under the hollowed-out oak tree. As they were nearing the end of their journey, Philip thought that he had been a real jerk to misjudge Scotty, and as they approached the opposite bank, Philip turned around to invite Scotty to join him and his frog friends for a spider hunt when he returned from caring for his dear Aunt Scarletta.

But before he could open his mouth to speak, Philip suddenly felt a terrible, penetrating sting deep in his back. His body went numb, and he struggled to stay above water as Scotty, laughing an evil laugh, lunged forward in the water and scurried up onto the bank. Try as he might, Philip could not regain control of his body because he was paralyzed from the poison. As he fought for his life, he cried out to Scotty, "I trusted you, Scotty! Why did you sting me?!?" Still laughing his awful laugh, Scotty called back, "Because I'm a scorpion, you fool. That's what I *do*!"

And with the final realization that Scotty the Scorpion was only doing what he was expected to do, poor, kind Philip the Frog sunk slowly into his watery grave.

Now I know what you're thinking: "Dr. Cortman, that's a *terrible* story!" And you're right, it is terrible, but that doesn't mean it's not true. Okay, it's not true, but that's beside the point. The point is that, for Erica, it took the story about Philip the Frog to realize what she later admitted she had known the whole time: that Carter was a cheater and that he was just doing what he was expected to do. Erica knew he was a cheater the night she helped him cheat on Stefani, and she had suspected for more than a year that he wasn't always being truthful, but she allowed herself to remain in a state of denial until finally she could deny it no more. And as painful as it may have been for her, to begin the healing process and move on from her feelings of betrayal and humiliation, Erica had to learn firsthand the painful lesson of Social Black Belt Truth N°9: You can trust people to be who they are, not who you want them to be.

Here are two simple facts. First, people do what makes sense to them, not necessarily what makes sense to us. Second, people do what makes them happy, not necessarily what makes us happy. These facts apply to me, and they apply to you. But they also apply to the people around you. In a perfect world, we would all be able to trust everyone blindly without fear of betrayal, exploitation, or disappointment. But the world's not perfect. Not even close. And not everyone shares the same values, beliefs, or expectations. For Erica, honesty and monogamy were essential elements in her relationship. Carter, however, simply did not place the same value on those expectations. Somewhere along the line, he gave himself permission to lie and cheat in relationships, and Erica—and Stefani—paid the price for it. She knew his reputation, and she suspected his dishonesty, but deep down she hoped that maybe he had changed, that maybe he would be different with her than he had been with all the others. Simply put, she had certain expectations of Carter, and she was wrong.

Different Types of Trust

When you think about it, you already know that you can't trust all people all the time. Unless you grew up in a cave or a bubble, surely someone has lied to you or betrayed you before. But that doesn't mean you don't trust *anyone,* does it? Surely there are people in your life who you know will keep things real with you, who won't lie to you or steal from you or stab you in the back. Or maybe there are people who you trust in some ways but not in others. For example, maybe you trust your best friend never to talk trash about you behind your back, but you definitely don't trust her to pick you up for school on time in the mornings. Or maybe you trust your younger sister to always keep your secrets confidential, but you don't trust her to not use your makeup without asking.

The point is you can trust people to be who they are, not who you want them to be. You might *want* your bestie to be in your driveway at 7:05 a.m. like she always says she will be, but you already know that 7:25 is a little more realistic. You might *want* your younger sister to keep her grubby little hands off your eyeliner, but deep down you know that that's just not going to happen. Sure, you might be frustrated with people sometimes, but so what? I've got news for you: Sometimes they're frustrated with you! So rather than constantly stressing out over people not behaving the way *you* want them to behave, just accept them for who they are—the good and the bad.

But don't forget, as I discussed in Truth N°7, you can't change people. If people want to change themselves—gain new insights, develop healthier behaviors, etc.—that's fine, but they're going to have to do that on their own terms when it's right for them, not on your terms when it's right for you. In the meantime, you simply can't waste your time and energy expecting other people to live up to *your* standards or expectations. Instead, trust them to be who they are, and adjust yourself accordingly.

If Carter has a history of cheating, expect him to cheat again. If Scotty has a history of stabbing people in the back, watch your back. Ignoring Truth N°9—in other words, expecting people to be someone *other than who they are*—is only going to set you up for a lifetime of disappointment.

So What Can You Do?

Trusting people can be hard. Parents often bring their troubled teenagers to me concerned that their child has some bad habits—lying, skipping school, drug use, you name it. Many parents tell me similar stories: their child got caught doing something bad, was punished and stopped doing the bad thing, then started doing the bad thing again when the punishment was over. Naturally the parents are frustrated and disappointed when their child reverts to their old negative behaviors—but they shouldn't be surprised.

Nor should they give up. The child will change when doing something good makes more sense than doing something bad—in other words, when going to school makes more sense than skipping, or when telling the truth makes more sense than lying. In the meantime, however, parents should not be misled into believing something that isn't true. Past behaviors predict future behaviors, so parents shouldn't blindly trust their child simply because he or she promises not to do it again. The child must *earn* the parents' trust by establishing a *new* pattern of behaviors that will *eventually* allow people to trust them again.

And you should use the same approach. Trust people to be who they are—for better or for worse—and then trust your own judgment. If your girlfriend has never given you a reason to mistrust her, then don't mistrust her. If your best friend has never lied to you, then by all means, take what she says as the truth. But if someone has given you reasons to doubt their word or their intentions, especially if this behavior has been repeated numerous times, then be cautious. Do not set yourself up for disappointment over and over again by placing your trust in people who have proven they don't live up to their word. Instead, place trust in *yourself.* Trust that you know it can sometimes be risky to place faith in other people *and* that you are strong and smart enough to deal responsibly with the outcome, even if it isn't what you had hoped for. Trust that your girlfriend won't cheat on you, but also trust that if she does, you will be able to do what is best for you and come out stronger in the end.

Dealing with the Hurt:
Options for Action!

When you reach a place where you can trust your own judgement of others—in other words, when you know who they are and what to expect of them—then you'll be much better equipped to handle whatever comes your way. When people disappoint you—and they definitely will—you don't have to respond reflexively with anger, shock, or sadness. Next time someone breaks your trust or does what they promised they would never do again, don't let these powerful emotions take over you. You've got options! For example, you could:

 Choose to Ignore the Other Person's Behavior, Especially If It's Something Minor, It Was an Accident, or It's the First Time They've Acted That Way,

 Choose to Tell the Person That Their Behavior Is Hurtful and Unacceptable and That You Expect Them to Do Better Next Time,

 Choose to Forgive the Person, and Give Them Another Chance,

 Choose to Stop Trusting the Person, and Be on Your Emotional or Physical Guard Around Them Until They Regain Your Trust Through Repeated Trustworthy Actions,

 Or, If the Behavior Is Repeated or Especially Awful, Choose to Release Your Hurt and Anger, Then Cut the Person Out of Your Life.

Remember: You are under no obligation to keep toxic people in your life.

Ultimately, the choice is yours. And that's the key: It is *your choice.* As I said in Truth N°8, it is up to *you* to create boundaries, so when it comes to giving people your trust, you have to know where to draw the line. Only you know the people and the situations in your life, but please know that you have the power to choose whether to trust someone and keep them around or to not trust them and cut them loose. Just don't expect them to be someone they're not.

Hope for Redemption

I'd like to end this chapter on a positive note. In some cases, people *do* change. If there were no possible way people could ever improve themselves, you wouldn't be reading this book, and I wouldn't have written it. You've gotten this far, presumably, because you want to make yourself better in some way. Well, the same goes for other people. Sometimes people *do* learn from their mistakes and fundamentally change who they are. Isn't that the goal?

There's an old saying that you've probably heard: "Once a cheater, always a cheater." Well I've got news for you: This simply isn't true. Sometimes people who have been unfaithful in the past do stop cheating. Or lying, or stealing, or using hard drugs. I have a patient who used to do all of the above. He was a drug user, a thief, a compulsive liar—and he cheated on women constantly. Today, however, he's a model citizen—sober, honest, and completely faithful. Over the years he hurt many people, but when he began to see all the hurt he was causing—and all the good people who no longer wanted him around—he made a commitment to change. It may have taken a long time for the people he hurt to place their trust in him again, but again and again he made sure that his positive words were backed up by positive deeds until, eventually, his old deceptive habits were replaced by new honest ones. Of course, the people he hurt did not *forget* all the awful things he did in the past, but over time they forgave him and began to see that he had truly changed for the better.

Try the following exercises to help you work through your past experiences with betrayal and to begin to trust people to be who they really are.

———

TAKE CHANCES AND TRUST YOUR JUDGEMENT

Here is a hard truth: There is no foolproof way to ever know if you can truly trust someone to live up to their word. But that doesn't mean you should never trust people. Most people are good most of the time, and everyone screws up on occasion—even you. If people violate your trust, you have options. You can forgive them—or not—or give them a second chance—or not. The choice is yours. But either way, you don't have to let your happiness depend on other peoples' behavior. If someone betrays you or lies to you, *they're* the fool, not you. Expecting the best of others doesn't make you weak; it makes you good and honest and trusting. Taking others at their word is a choice—a choice to trust in them *and* to trust in yourself, specifically, in your ability to be smart about whom to trust and when, and in your ability to take appropriate actions when you need to.

EXERCISES

———

After reading about Truth N°9, you now know what you've probably known all along: people will sometimes let you down. But you should also know that you can prepare yourself for the occasional let-down by setting realistic expectations about people based on what you already know about them and that you have options for how to move on from these disappointments when they arise. The following exercises will help you analyze past violations of your trust, set realistic expectations of others, and put a plan in place for the next time your trust is violated.

① When Has Your Trust Been Violated in the Past?

While this exercise might dredge up some old feelings of anger, hurt, disappointment, or betrayal, it's important to think about a time when you expected someone to behave in a way that defies their character and were then hurt when they turned out to be exactly who you knew they were the whole time. For example, maybe you were really hoping your alcoholic aunt would show up to your big dance recital sober like she promised she would, but were then devastated and embarrassed when she showed up to the event drunker than you've ever seen her. Answer the following questions to help you process this disappointment.

Who is a person in your life who you wished behaved differently, you've given second or third chances to, or gets your hopes up that they will change only to let you down again?

_____

What specific action or behavior did this person do to you that you once forgave?

_____

_____

_____

Despite their bad behavior, _why_ did you forgive them? In other words, what was going through your mind that allowed you to give them a second chance?

_____

_____

_____

When you gave this person a second (or third, or fourth, etc.) chance, what, exactly did it look like?

_____

_____

_____

Then, what did they do with this second chance? Did they act badly again, or did they correct their behavior and never do it again? How did it make you feel?

_____

_____

_____

Finally, looking back, what signs were there that his person could have been expected to behave exactly the way they did, instead of the way you _hoped_ they would?

_____

_____

_____

2 The Frankenstein Fantasy

Thinking of this same person, now imagine you have the ability to give this person a personality makeover so they will behave any way you want them to. If you could change this person into your perfect version of them, what things would you change, and why? Be specific.

_____

_____

_____

_____

_____

_____

_____

3 The Frankenstein Fantasy Part 2

Thinking of this fantasy monster you've created, answer the following three questions.

Is it possible this person you know could ever become this perfect version you've created of them? If yes, explain how. If no, explain why this is unrealistic.

_____

_____

_____

Assuming the person cannot realistically be changed to your fantasy person entirely, what are *some* of the ways this person *could* change, and what would they need to do to make this happen?

_____

_____

_____

Finally, what are some ways you could help this person change for the better without allowing them to hurt you, betray you, or make you look or feel like a fool for believing in them?

_____

_____

_____

4 Trusting Yourself to Do What You Need to Do... *FOR YOU!*

This final step might be the hardest part, the part when you need to do some real soul searching. This, as they say, is where the rubber meets the road. Now you need to pre-pare yourself for the very real possibility that this person will *not* change in the ways you hope. You need to have a plan in place next time they behave the way you expect them to, not the way you want them to. So, next time this person betrays you or violates your trust, will you:

Choose to ignore this behavior? Why or why not?

_____

_____

_____

Choose to tell the person that their behavior is hurtful and unacceptable and that you expect them to do better next time? If so, what, exactly will you say?

_____

_____

_____

Choose to forgive this person and give them another chance? Why or why not?

_____

_____

_____

Choose to stop trusting the person and be on your emotional or physical guard around them until they regain your trust through repeated trustworthy actions? Explain what would have to happen for them to regain this trust.

_____

_____

_____

Choose to release your hurt and anger, then cut the person out of your life? How will you do this, and how will your life change as a consequence?

_____

_____

_____

TRUTH N° 10

Time Doesn't Heal All Pain; We Heal Ourselves by Learning to Let Pain Go

It had already been the most painful week of Tommy's young life, but today would be the day that would stick with him forever. For what seemed an eternity, one by one, friends, family, and many people Tommy had never seen before—and many he would never see again— paraded past the coffin of his father to pay their respects. Some of the mourners bowed their heads, silently said a prayer, and moved on quickly to take their seats in the back of the viewing room. Some wept openly, dabbing tissues to their eyes and noses and sniffling quietly as they stood in groups hugging one another. Others simply stared in disbelief at the cold corpse of a healthy man who had died unexpectedly in the prime of his life. Tommy's grandmother threw herself on the casket and wailed uncontrollably, loudly, painfully. "Mommy loves you," she cried, "Mommy loves you!" Spry and fresh just the week before, she looked to Tommy like she had aged 20 years overnight as she hobbled away unsteadily, trembling and gasping for breath.

And then there was Tommy's sister, Meghan. Just 8 years old, she hadn't cried and had barely said a word all week. On the day of the funeral, she stood silently for hours at the head of her father's casket, stroking his hair calmly and whispering in his ear, just as she had done when he was alive. When the people from the funeral parlor began to remove the flowers and close the casket, Meghan passed out cold and fell to the floor. Completely limp, she was carried to the car by her uncles and taken home to bed, where she slept, whimpering, for the next 24 hours.

Along with his uncles, grandfather, and 10-year-old brother Devin, Tommy, now the man of the house at just 16, stared straight ahead as he helped carry his father's heavy casket the short distance from the funeral parlor to the burial site. And though it was killing him inside, Tommy refused to cry as the casket was lowered into the ground. Shielding himself behind dark sunglasses, Tommy stared into the distance as people wept and threw dirt and flowers into the grave. *This is life,* he thought coldly. *Time to move on.*

The Hard Truth About Pain

If you're like most people, you probably assume that things get better with time, that, with each day that passes, the pain you experience—from loss, betrayal, abandonment, abuse—eases just a little bit. And to a certain extent, this is true. Mostly, the more time that passes after an event, the less painful and immediate the event feels. In fact, if this weren't the case, how could any of us go on living our lives? Can you imagine what life would be like if the pain we experience after the breakup of a long relationship or the death of a loved one never went away and never got any better? The emotional weight of adding pain, on top of pain, on top of pain, on top of pain—without any relief at all—would be unbearable.

In reality, time does help us move past some traumatic events. You may have fond memories of your childhood pet, but you are not still an emotional wreck 15 years after its death. It was awful at first, then just kind of sad, then something you accepted and moved on from. Most days—in fact, most weeks or months, even—you probably don't think of your childhood pet at all. Come to think of it, in the moment I am writing this paragraph, I realize that I have not given a single thought to Cleon—a beloved three-legged golden retriever who was euthanized when I was 6—in about 30 years. When Cleon died, I cried for days, but time passed and I moved on. Could you imagine if I were still bawling my eyes out decades later over the death of my childhood pet? I'd need a psychologist.

But just because time allows us to heal from some losses does not mean time heals all wounds. If my child were brutally murdered, for example—and it pains me to even think about—I would never "get over it" like I did the loss of Cleon. In time, the *shock* of the event might lessen, but 10 years from now—50 years from now—I would still love him and miss him just the same and would still become deeply emotional when I thought about him. There is simply no amount of time that could pass that would close that gaping wound in my heart.

But even if I experienced a loss as tragic as the one I've just described—which, by the way, people around the world do every day, unfortunately—I could still go on living my life seeking happiness, purpose, and fulfillment after an appropriate—and necessary—period of mourning. In other words, this event, as tragic as it would be, would not be an excuse to give up or spend the rest of my life in total misery. What would make my healing possible, though, is not the mere passage of time. Instead, it would be the incredible amount of psychological and emotional *work* I would need to do to begin to heal *myself.*

And this is where Social Black Belt Truth N°10 comes into play. Healing is not a passive activity that "just happens" over time because time, by itself, does not heal pain. Healing is an *active* process, one that requires immense strength to push through, so it is only through *processing* pain and learning to let it go that we are able to heal enough to properly move on with our lives.

But let's return to Tommy for a few minutes. Tommy came to see me when he was 21, five years after the death of his father. When we spoke, Tommy was always calm, polite, respectful, and very easy to talk to. He was clean cut, handsome, and in very good shape. And he had a lot to be proud of. He had graduated high school with honors the year after his father died and was now only a year away from graduating college with a degree in engineering—a degree he said suited him because of its usefulness and precision. On the surface, Tommy seemed completely fine, a model citizen any mother would be proud of. But I have decades of experience in reading people, and I could tell something was up. Plus, people generally don't make appointments to see a psychologist when everything in their lives is perfect. So even though he was a bit hesitant at first, Tommy and I quickly got down to business.

Despite Tommy's outward appearance of ease, steadiness, and general likeability, he was a total mess inside. In the few months following Tommy's father's death, Tommy's mother became emotionally unstable and deeply depressed. Sure, it was natural for her to be very sad, but she also drank a lot, slept a lot, and stopped taking care of herself. At first, Tommy gave her room to grieve in her own way—even if it was a bit unhealthy—but in the five years since, she has never really recovered. She lost her job because she was so unsteady, and she nearly lost their home. If it hadn't been for Tommy's taking on a part-time job immediately after his father's death, and full-time job when he turned 18—in addition to going to school full time—Tommy and his entire family would have been out on the streets a long time ago.

Of course, all of this was hard for Tommy—really hard. He pushed and pushed, but the effort to maintain work, school, bills, and parenting—not only his siblings, but his mother, too—was taking a toll on him. To keep order in his life, Tommy became emotionally cold and worked obsessively. He ran his siblings like a drill sergeant runs recruits—showing no love but demanding results. Always exhausted and constantly overwhelmed, Tommy became angry—and sometimes physically threatening. He intimidated his mother and terrified his siblings. Deep down, Tommy knew this was not who he was or who he wanted to be, but it was who he had to become to keep his family and his life from falling apart—at least that's what he told himself.

Tommy's breaking point, and the event that brought him to my office, happened the week before we met. While Tommy was at work, he received a message from his former high school principal saying that his brother Devin, now 15, had not been in school for three days. Knowing Devin was not sick, Tommy called Devin and then his mother, but neither picked up their phones. Worried something was seriously wrong, Tommy left work and rushed home to see what was going on. What he found made him snap.

Instead of going to school for the past three days, Tommy's brother had been skipping with some friends, staying home to smoke weed and play video games all day. If this weren't bad enough, Tommy's mom was home and knew the boys were there—she had just been too hungover to care. Tommy was furious. Here he was, working more than 40 hours a week, going to school full time, paying all the bills, and doing everything he could to keep Devin and Meghan on track, and she had the nerve to be in bed all day knowing full well her 15-year-old was skipping school and using drugs—in the house! Tommy screamed at his mother. He got in her face. When he got too close, she tried to slap him,

but Tommy grabbed her arm and pushed her to the floor. Devin tried to intervene, but Tommy gave it to him, too, and "beat the crap out of him," as he told me. Tommy stormed out of the house and didn't return for three days.

When I asked Tommy to describe how his father's sudden death five years ago had affected him and his family, he had a lot to say about his mother's checking out, his brother's rebelliousness, and his sister's frequent crying and long bouts of silence—and about the immense number of responsibilities he had had to take on to keep their lives in order— but he had almost nothing to say about himself. "I'm fine," he said. "A little tired maybe, but fine." When I reminded Tommy that I'm a clinical psychologist and not a mattress salesman—in other words, people don't call my office for a counseling session when they're just "a little tired"—Tommy confessed to me that he was at his breaking point. He barely ate, slept, or had any time for himself. He had few friends in college and hadn't dated anyone since his father died. "No time," he said. All he did was work, study, take care of the family,and repeat. Day in, day out, for five years straight. He was physically exhausted.

When I asked about his emotional state since his father's death, he said the same thing he had said when I asked about his friends—"No time." "Come again?" I said. And he repeated: "I don't have time to be emotional. I have too much to do." And *this*, I realized, was the root of Tommy's problem. In the five years since his father died, Tommy had not had any time to grieve properly and begin to heal. Life had just thrown too much at him, and he had to push his own feelings deep down below the surface where they could not get in the way of his responsibilities.

In a way, I had to hand it to Tommy. He could have chosen his mother's way of emotional suppression—drinking, sleeping, crying all day, ignoring responsibilities—but he chose the opposite. Not too many people can say they've accomplished as much as Tommy had at such a young age and with so little help. But at what cost?

Tommy told me that work and school helped him to avoid thinking about his father, and when thoughts of his dad did creep in, Tommy pushed them down and took on a task—homework, a project at school—whatever it took to keep his mind busy. Tommy never spoke to anyone about his father's death—not his mother, and not even his siblings, who desperately needed his emotional guidance. He never wrestled with his own feelings of loss in a healthy way. Instead, he allowed anger and obsession to settle in. Eventually, these feelings became his shield against the possibility of processing his pain, and he never looked back and never changed course. Something had to give. Tommy could not go on like this forever.

Like Tommy, many of my other patients come to me after being unable to simply "get over" traumatic or sad events. Some, like Tommy, have lost loved ones to sudden deaths—murders, suicides, drug overdoses, car accidents—and others have been raped, beaten, abandoned, or robbed at gunpoint. While every person's situation is unique, they all share something in common: deep pain of one kind or another. In almost every case, no matter the cause of the pain, I explain to my patients that healing is a complicated process and that time alone will not ease their hurt. I tell them that if they just sit around, waiting for things to magically improve, nothing will happen. In many cases, if left unaddressed, the emotional pain gets much worse and causes even more problems. Like a wound that might get infected if left untreated, pain should be addressed as early as possible so it doesn't get worse over time.

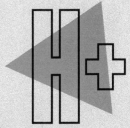

TIP N°10

HEAL

To help my patients process and move past their painful experiences and memories, I guide them through the following five-step process. In some cases patients begin to feel better in mere days; in other cases the process takes much longer. What's crucial, though, is that my patients—and you—follow the process and stick to it. While it may be difficult at times, working through the five steps is necessary to begin to recover from pain and trauma and move toward a place of emotional well-being. The first three steps involve facing the pain head on; the fourth step involves letting it go; the fifth involves changing your thinking so you can change the way you feel. Let's take a look.

1. Remembering

Some people think avoiding pain is easier if they simply try to forget about what caused it in the first place, but trying to forget that you fell off your bike doesn't change the fact that you have a broken arm in need of immediate medical attention. In other words, just because you don't think about the painful event doesn't mean the issues it's causing in your life will go away. Tommy tried to forget about his father's sudden passing, and it affected him deeply. Ignoring his father's death didn't bring him back, and it didn't help Tommy at all. The truth is that to move past the pain, you must first return to what caused it.

Have you ever seen or heard a tea kettle boil? Like a tea kettle, when you ignore painful events and try to push them out of your mind, they begin to create a sort of pressure inside you. And like a tea kettle, if you don't find some way to release this pressure in a healthy way, eventually you'll scream or crack—or both. This is what happened to Tommy. He ignored his pain for so long that, well, he sort of cracked up at the end.

Sometimes the memories are so painful that the mind forces them down so deeply that you actually *don't* remember them. It's your mind's defense mechanism, a way of protecting you from what you may not be ready to process. In psychology, we call these memories *repressed memories.* Repressed memories are generally of very traumatic events like prolonged sexual assault, a very serious accident, or a violent attack. This was not the case for Tommy, fortunately, but many people's experiences are that extreme.

Either way, the key to working through these memories in a healthy way is to talk to someone you trust completely. This person could be a close friend, a parent, a teacher, or, in some cases, a therapist like me. When you find someone like this, you should feel a sense of security, not judgement, when you talk through the pain. Talking about these memories will likely be painful, but this process is necessary. Like removing a bandaid or a bad tooth, the process may hurt in the moment, but the result is very rewarding—necessary, even. Living your life free of ongoing emotional pain is like recovery for your heart and mind. The sooner you start to heal, the sooner you can move forward mostly free of needless pain and suffering.

2. Feeling

Of course, simply remembering the bad thing that happened to you is not enough to heal the pain. If that were the case, the memory wouldn't hurt in the first place. To truly let go, you must also *feel* what hurts you. Many people avoid feeling the pain of their traumatic or difficult events by numbing themselves with drugs, alcohol, sex, shopping, or other addictions. Others, like Tommy, avoid feeling their pain by becoming fixated, even obsessed, with various goals or by turning off their emotions entirely and becoming cold and robotic. Of course, robots don't feel pain, but they also don't feel joy. So to become someone who experiences joy again, you must first feel, process, then release the pain.

Unresolved feelings are feelings that have not been fully processed. For example, if someone says to you, "It sounds like you've never really dealt with your father's death" or "You're still pretty angry about Jason's stealing from you," they're commenting on unresolved feelings. Even though the events may be in the distant past, the feelings they cause inside you remain powerful forces in your life. Sure, like Tommy, you might think you're "tough enough" to deal with the pain, but why would you want to carry all that hurt around with you in the first place? Why not move through the process now so you can leave it in the past where it belongs? The longer you hang on to it, the more damage it's going to cause you, and the worse you're going to feel.

3. Expressing

Here's where some of the real work begins. Now that you're remembering your trauma and feeling the pain, shame, or fear that it caused you, what, exactly, are you supposed to *do* about it? Well, you have to give a voice to it.

It's not enough to *feel* the pain—heck, that's the part you're trying to get rid of, isn't it? You have to *express* it. For many people this part can be difficult because giving voice to the pain makes it more real—something they generally try to avoid. In some cases, expressing your pain may mean telling others something you may have kept entirely to yourself for a long, long time, and this can be quite difficult. When Ke'Andre's girlfriend cheated on him and only he knew about it, he swallowed that betrayal and never told anyone. Instead, he became hardened inside and mean to people—especially women—as a defense against allowing anyone to betray him. He was also ashamed and embarrassed, and he just couldn't bring himself to say it out loud to anyone—not even his girlfriend. He was so hurt by what he read in her text messages that he couldn't even confront her about it. It was after two years of depression and hard-hearted behavior that he finally came to me to move past his betrayal. For Ke'Andre, just saying the words, "My girlfriend slept with another guy" was the most difficult part—but also the most important. If he hadn't confronted his pain—and expressed it—he would never have fully recovered from it.

What your particular issue is will likely dictate how and to whom you express your pain. For some people, a trusted friend or relative does the trick. For some it's a therapist. And for others it's a support group. It doesn't matter who you talk to, just talk. Have you ever heard someone say, "I need to get something off my chest"? Maybe you've said it yourself. This is what expressing your pain is all about. For many people, talking about what hurts them is enough. For others, writing a letter helps. Sometimes there are things you can say on paper that you just can't find the strength to say out loud, and that's okay. It's not about *how* you express yourself; it's simply that you *do* it that matters. Also, while you *can* give the letter to the person who caused your trauma, you certainly don't have to. In fact, in some cases—for example, if you're not allowed to have contact with the person—it might be best not to deliver the letter at all. In these cases, the letter is just a form of expression you keep to yourself. Either way,

writing a letter or speaking directly to a person you're comfortable and safe with are an important part of the healing process.

When expressing your trauma—either on paper or verbally—try to address these four core components. First, simply state what happened. As they used to say back in the dinosaur times, "Just the facts, ma'am." Second, explain how the incident made you feel at the time. Third, express how the event has impacted you since it occurred. It doesn't matter if your trauma happened last week or ten years ago; if the pain is still impacting you, you need to say so. Finally, try to figure out a way to let the pain go and adjust your ways of thinking. For most people, these last two steps are the hardest. Lucky for you, I've got a few suggestions for how to do them!

4. Releasing

One of the easiest ways to release your pain—but also one of the hardest—is to forgive the person who caused it. When I say it's one of the easiest ways, I mean that you will find it easier to move on from the pain if you no longer have hard feelings against the person who caused it. When I say it's one of the hardest ways, I mean that it can sometimes be very hard to forgive the people who have hurt you. One way to forgive someone who has hurt you is to try to see things from their perspective. By this, I do not mean you should try to excuse their behavior. I mean you should try to think of what may have happened in their life that may have caused them to do what they did. There is a difference between an excuse and a reason, and sometimes finding the reason someone may have hurt you can help you forgive them. Let me give you an example.

When Gavin was 6 years old, his father abandoned him and his mother. Prior to his leaving, Gavin's father used to hit Gavin—a lot. After every time this happened, Gavin's father would say things like, "Daddy's sorry he hit you" or "Daddy's sorry he was so mean to you." He used to promise Gavin he wouldn't hit him anymore, but then he would do it again a few days or weeks later. One day Gavin's father hit him especially hard—much harder than a spanking or slap on the hand—and Gavin's mother told him to leave until he could get his anger under control. He left the very next day, and he didn't return for ten years.

Understandably, when Gavin came to see me a few months after his dad came back into his life, he was really mixed up about it. One the one hand, he was glad to see his father after so long. On the other hand, he was a little scared of him because of all the memories he had of him being violent. Most of all, however, Gavin was really angry that his dad had just disappeared for ten whole years. That was ten years of basketball games, ten years of school plays, and ten years of watching his mom cry alone at the kitchen table.

When I suggested to Gavin that forgiving his father might be a way to release the pain that his feelings of abandonment had caused, his reaction, understandably, was "Not a chance!" Eventually, though, Gavin came around. He knew that to feel better inside he would have to release his anger and pain. Most of all—and this was the hardest thing for him to admit—he wanted a relationship with his father. The question, then, wasn't whether Gavin should forgive him, but how he could.

I told Gavin that one way to forgive his father would be to try to see things from his father's perspective—to see why he might have done what he did. I asked Gavin to tell me everything he knew about his father, especially about what his father's childhood was like. Of course, Gavin barely knew the guy, so he had to talk to his mom to get a lot of the information. It turns out that Gavin's grandfather, whom Gavin never knew, was a very angry man who used to beat all of his children—especially Gavin's father— severely and often. So severely, in fact, that Gavin's father almost died from one of his father's beatings. When Gavin's father was 16, his dad pointed a gun at him and told him he should have killed him when he was a baby. A few weeks later, Gavin's grandfather left his family and never returned.

Gavin admitted that his mother had told him that his father hated being beaten as a child and had never fully recovered from his scars—neither the physical ones nor the psychological ones—and as a result, Gavin's father developed his own issues with anger and violence. When Gavin was 6, it had been only ten years since his grandfather had beaten his father, pointed the gun at him, and abandoned him. In other words, when Gavin's father was beating Gavin, he was still suffering from the trauma from his *own* childhood—just as Gavin was with me.

It turns out that Gavin's father left because he thought it was in Gavin's best interest for him not to be around. Gavin's father hated the fact that he hit his son, and he felt guilty every time he did it. He knew from experience that it was wrong to hit a child, and here he was doing the very same things to his own child that his father had done to him. In the end, he felt it was better for Gavin to be with only his mother until he got his life straightened out. As strange as it may sound, Gavin's father saw leaving his son not as an act of abandonment, but as an act of love and protection.

When I asked Gavin if he could see how that kind of upbringing might explain why his father left him when he was 6, Gavin admitted that he could. When I asked Gavin if, in light of this new understanding, he might be able to forgive his father as a way to help *himself* heal, I could sense the anger lift from Gavin's shoulders. Seeing his father for what he had *been through* instead of what he had *done* helped Gavin forgive him and let go of some of his anger and pain.

Here are two more quick points to keep in mind about forgiveness: First, there are two kinds of forgiveness. The first kind of forgiveness includes reconciliation, while the second kind does not. If your friend gets in your face and pushes you in front of everyone during lunch, you can choose to forgive him and give him a second chance, or you can choose to forgive him and stop being his friend. It is up to you if, when, and under what conditions you forgive someone.

Second, while it may seem as if forgiveness is a gift you give to the person who hurt you (which, of course, it is), it is really a gift you give to *yourself.* When you forgive someone, you give yourself permission to move on from the pain they have caused you. When you forgive someone, you are telling them that you will no longer allow their misdeeds to hold you back from being your happiest self.

At this point you might be thinking, *But Dr. Cortman, I* can't *forgive that person. What she did was too horrible.* And you're right: Sometimes offering forgiveness is hard— really hard. And maybe you just can't bring yourself to do it yet. On the other hand, many people eventually do forgive, even when they think they never will. Sometimes it takes time—lots of time, even—and that's okay. You can forgive only when you are truly ready to.

If you aren't quite ready to forgive someone, that doesn't mean you have to carry the weight of all that pain around with you. You can still release it in other ways and move on with your life. Here are just a few suggestions to help you let go of what's keeping you down, even if you aren't quite ready to forgive the ones who've hurt you.

ARTISTIC EXPRESSION

Many people struggling to release trauma or deep emotional pain find relief in creating art. Of course, art takes many forms: drawing, painting, sculpting, making music, dancing, writing poetry or stories, and more. Marcia writes poems to release the pain of her mother's imprisonment, Enrique dedicates his time to writing lyrics and producing hip-hop beats to make sense of his older brother's heroin addiction, and Michael carves wood sculptures like the ones he and his father used to carve together before his dad committed suicide three years ago.

Here's the best thing about the benefits of using art to release your pain: you can be as awesome as Picasso or as terrible as I am and still receive the same benefits.

Art is whatever you think it is. So what if your paintings are terrible? Mine are, too. If you feel good when you're creating them, keep doing it. Eventually you'll get better, but that's not the point. The point is that you'll be engaging in a healthy and safe activity that makes you feel good and proud, not a harmful one that makes you feel worse. So go ahead, find your passion. Explore the arts. You'll be happy you did.

PRAYER AND RELIGION

One thing that prayer and religion have in common with trauma and pain is that they are all deeply personal. No one's relationship with God is quite the same as anyone else's, just as no one's pain is quite the same as anyone else's. These experiences are unique every time. Even Chadwick and Alton, identical twins raised in the same religion and affected by loss of the same cousin to cancer, have different relationships with God and have different emotional reactions to their cousin's death. Chadwick feels close to God and goes to church every Sunday. When his cousin died, he sought advice during weekly talks with his pastor and processed his pain through the closeness he felt to his youth group on their monthly volunteer missions. Alton, on the other hand, doesn't attend church very often and does not participate in the youth group. He does, however, feel a close personal relationship to God, and he prays often. In fact, he describes God as someone he can talk to any time, any place—and the release he feels from these conversations helps him feel connected to something meaningful when he starts to feel especially sad about his cousin.

The reality is it doesn't matter what religion you are or if you have no organized religion at all. You can be Christian, Jewish, Muslim, Jain, Hindu, Buddhist, Rastafarian, Taoist, or anything else. Maybe you don't consider yourself religious but are simply spiritual. This is fine, too. If prayer or a relationship with a religious organization helps you cope with your issues, then by all means, pray away.

If a personal interpretation of a spiritual force gets you through the day without constantly being bogged down by your past experiences, tap into it. If it's all good, then it's all good. Got it?

PHILOSOPHY

Of course, not everyone is religious in the traditional sense, and many people believe God and the spiritual realm don't exist at all. For agnostics—those who are unsure about the nature of God—and atheists—those who believe God does not exist—philosophy may be helpful. While religion and philosophy can be different in some ways, they also have a lot in common. Both are deeply personal, and both offer many options for exploration. For example, maybe you've never heard of German philosopher Friedrich Nietzsche, but I'd be willing to bet you've heard one of his most famous quotations: "That which does not kill me makes me stronger." Sure, the pain sucks, but everyone goes through it at one point or another. The question is, will you let it kill you, or will you be stronger in the end for having gone through it? Nietzsche is just one of thousands of philosophers you might benefit from reading. The Stoics, for example, believed that pain is inevitable, but allowing it to tear you down is not. I feel the same way, and with a little hard work and a change in mindset, hopefully you will, too.

One last point about religion and philosophy: Sometimes young people find them intimidating or hard to understand. Often the texts are thousands of years old, and the ideas can be a little complicated. But don't be turned off by something just because it is difficult at first. If you had done that when you were little, you wouldn't know how to tie your shoes or ride a bike today. Approach religion and philosophy at your own pace. Don't take on more than you can handle, and don't rush the process. Read what makes sense to you, and things will become clearer as you gain practice and experience. You weren't popping wheelies the day you took off your training wheels, were you? Methinks not.

SUBLIMATION

Another way to help release your emotional pain is through sublimation. Now, I know what you're thinking: *Another big word that doesn't make any sense.* But it's actually really simple. Sublimation is basically a way of taking a bad situation and making it into something positive—in other words, turning that frown upside down. One of the most famous examples of someone who processed pain through sublimation is Candy Lightner. In 1980, Lightner's daughter Cari was killed when she was hit by a car driven by someone who was drunk. While Candy was undoubtedly very sad about the senseless death of her daughter, she was also very angry. But rather than allowing her sadness and anger to consume her, Lightner turned her negative energy into a positive cause: she formed Mothers Against Drunk Driving, or MADD, an organization whose mission is to raise awareness about the dangers of drunk driving, so no other mother will ever experience the pain she did. This process of channelling your pain into something positive is sublimation.

So, how can you use your experiences to make a difference in your life and the lives of other people? If you were abused as a child, maybe you can volunteer at a youth shelter, reading books to children or playing games with them to make them feel loved and safe. If your grandmother died of breast cancer, maybe you can start a fundraising campaign at your school during Breast Cancer Awareness month or participate in a Susan G. Komen Race for the Cure event. Whatever the source of your pain, one sure way to help alleviate its impact is to help ensure others don't have to experience it, too. Volunteering feels good. Helping others feels good. So get out there and turn that pain into something you can be proud of. Ya' know, sublimate.

5. Changing Your Thinking

If there's one lesson that I hope you take away from this book, it's that you can change your life by changing your thinking. At the risk of sounding repetitive, I'd like to revisit this concept one last time. As you may recall from the first Truth, the way you think impacts the way you feel, so if you want to change the way you feel, you have to change the way you think. Of course, this is not something you can achieve by simply snapping your fingers or wishing it would "just happen." You have to put in the work.

When it comes to releasing pain, changing your thinking means creating a life plan—one that doesn't involve allowing yourself to be dragged down by past experiences. In other words, releasing pain doesn't just mean saying goodbye to the past; it means saying hello to the future. To grow into your best self, you must learn to replace the negative things that have come before with positive things you *want* to experience and feel. When you release the bad, you embrace the good. Did your dog die? Mourn for an appropriate time, then adopt another one. Did your boyfriend leave you? Cry your eyes out, then spend more time with your friends until another lucky one comes along.

Of course, not every loss or source of pain is that simple to replace or overcome. If I were to suggest, for example, "Your mom died? Get a new one!" you would have every right to close this book right now and store it permanently in the nearest trash receptacle or fireplace. Some things simply cannot be replaced. In these cases, the healing cannot come in the form of a new puppy or boyfriend. Instead, it must come from within.

So, shift your focus. Find your purpose. Give yourself permission to be happy and to live the best life you can. Your time on this earth is limited, so why waste one more minute of it? If you allow the pain and trauma of your past to define your future, you are stealing from yourself. When you see an opportunity to improve your life and choose not to pursue it, you are, in a sense, victimizing *yourself*—and this you cannot blame on anyone else. Instead, accept what happened to you, process it, and let it go. The past cannot be changed, but what happens to you today and tomorrow and every day after that is completely up to you. Will you let your traumatic experiences control you, or will you become better, stronger, and more resilient because of them? Will you choose life? Will you choose happiness? The decision is yours, my young friend. Choose wisely.

———

EXERCISES

___

For many people, Truth N°10 may be the hardest to work through since it usually involves reliving some painful experiences you'd probably rather forget, but moving on requires work—often painful work—and the reward is definitely worth the effort. The following exercises are designed to help you remember, feel, express, and release your pain and, finally, to change the way you think about these past incidents. Remember these exercises as other painful experiences occur in your life, as they certainly will. We hope that with these tools, you will find yourself actively pursuing your emotional recovery and happiness, rather than waiting for it to magically appear over time.

① Remember When...?

In order to release the pain you feel inside, you must first be aware of what is causing it. Take a minute to describe something that happened in your past that you still feel impacted by and would like to move on from. For this exercise, just state what happened.

_____

_____

_____

_____

② How Does It Feel?

Now that you have identified an event, describe how it has made you feel. You may want to describe both how you felt right after the event and how it has made you feel since. Did you feel hurt, betrayed, scared, or unloved? How about now? Do you struggle with feelings of abandonment, neglect, or fear? Do you have trust issues? Do you lose sleep or not take care of yourself as you should? In as much detail as you can, describe the emotional impact of the event you described in Exercise 1.

_____

_____

_____

_____

3 Express Yourself

For this exercise, create a list of people you trust, people you know you can talk to when times get hard. These people may be friends, family members, teachers, coaches, or other people in the community. The purpose of this exercise is simply to identify all the people in your life you can turn to when the pain inside feels especially raw. Write down as many names as you can think of. If it's just one or two, fine. If it's more, even better.

When you're finished, select the person you think you might turn to first, and write a short script you can use to approach them to discuss your painful issue. For example, Angelica came up with the following short script to talk through her issues with her best friend, Tiger: "Tiger, can I talk to you for a minute? Something's been bothering me for a while, and I really need to talk to someone I trust. You're my best friend, and I feel pretty comfortable expressing my feelings to you." See? Pretty simple. Now you try it.

List of Names

1. _____   6. _____

2. _____   7. _____

3. _____   8. _____

4. _____   9. _____

5. _____   10. _____

Script for Your Approach

_____

_____

_____

4 Let It Go, Let It Go

This next activity has several phases. While it might be difficult at first, once you get past the hard parts, things only get better from there. First, take a few minutes to think about the person who hurt you. Specifically, try to think about *why* they hurt you. To be clear, I am not asking you to excuse this person's behavior; I'm asking you to think about what he or she might have experienced in life that may be a reason for it. While you may not be ready for forgiveness yet, developing a sense of empathy—even for the ones who have hurt you the most— is the first step in that process. And remember: While forgiveness may be a relief to the other person, it is first and foremost a gift you give to yourself. So, take a few minutes to jot down some reasons the other person may have hurt you—even if what they did was very bad—so you'll be one step closer to, well, letting it all go.

_____

_____

_____

_____

_____

_____

_____

_____

_____

_____

Okay, now that you've considered why the other person hurt you, you must next consider what it would take for you to forgive him or her. I understand that forgiveness may take a while, and that's fine. You get there when you get there. So if time is what you need, write it down. Also consider whether you might be willing to forgive the person if he or she offered a sincere apology, showed you changed behavior, or repaired what was damaged. If the person is no longer living, or if you have no contact with the person who hurt you, what changes need to take place *in you* before you are willing to forgive? If you're not in a place where you can even imagine forgiveness yet, that's okay. Some pain is very fresh and very deep, and forgiveness is a long way off. Maybe skip this part for now and come back to it when you're ready. Otherwise, take a few minutes to describe what your forgiveness might require.

_____

_____

_____

_____

_____

_____

_____

_____

_____

_____

Now comes the fun part. This next step is where you really get to explore who you are and what you love to do. After you've experienced heartache or trauma, it's important to find creative and relaxing ways to express yourself. Consider the options from this chapter: artistic expression, prayer, philosophy, and sublimation. Which do you find most appealing, and why? If you had the opportunity—which you do, by the way—which of these activities would you engage in to help relieve some of that hurt you're feeling? Will you create art? If so, what kind, and what of? Will you pray or read philosophy? Tell me about it. Will you improve the lives of others similarly impacted by trauma by volunteering or starting an awareness campaign? What cause will you focus on, and how will you do your part to fix it? If you've never done any of these activities, that's fine too. Feel free to do a little internet research about how to get started, or talk to someone you know who is already involved. Whatever your path forward, take a few minutes to describe it here. Then, go do it!

_____

_____

_____

_____

_____

_____

_____

_____

_____

5 Think Different, Feel Different, Be Different

This last step is probably the most rewarding—and the
most important. After all, it doesn't matter how many
poems you write or hours you volunteer if inside you're
still stuck in negative ways of thinking. And, like anything
else, changing your thinking takes practice. When I first
met Gavin, he was understandably down about his abandonment. He used to say things like, "Maybe my dad was
angry because he didn't want to raise a kid," and, "My
dad's a real piece of crap." After a while though, Gavin
started to say things like, "I know it wasn't my fault my
dad left. I just wish he could've found some other way to
work through his issues besides leaving me." Now you
do the same thing. First, write down a negative thought
associated with your pain or trauma that you find playing on repeat when you feel especially sad. Then, try to
reframe your thought the way Gavin did. In other words,
try to shift your perspective from one that drags you
down to one that lifts you up. If you have several negative
thoughts stuck on shuffle mode, rework them all.

1. Negative Thought:

_____

_____

_____

Positive Thought:

_____

_____

_____

2. Negative Thought:

_____

_____

_____

Positive Thought:

_____

_____

_____

3. Negative Thought:

_____

_____

_____

Positive Thought:

_____

_____

_____

CONCLUSION

CHAPTER 11

CONCLUSION

Don't Wear the Belt. *Be* the Belt

Wow! Congratulations, you've made it to the final chapter! But you're not finished just yet. You still have a *liiiittle* more work to do before I can hand you that Social Black Belt. I hope after reading about the Ten Truths and working through the various exercises you're feeling a little bit better about some things that may have been bothering you before, but I bet you're also wondering how you can put these Truths into everyday practice. Well, here's the answer: *practice.* The more you practice these Truths, the more they will become part of your consciousness and, eventually, your subconscious. Over time, you will notice that you don't have to think about them so often. The more you practice them, the more they'll become part of the natural process of navigating your day-to-day life, sort of like muscle memory for athletes, or the instincts of an artist applying paint to a canvas. For example, maybe one day in the future, you will find yourself attracted to someone you know is not good for you—maybe they have a history of cheating or abuse toward their partners—and instead of giving yourself permission to be cheated on or abused, you'll give yourself permission to wait until someone worth your time comes along. Or maybe you'll find yourself feeling unusually angry about something, and you're not sure why. These Truths will help bring you some clarity.

I realize I'm making this sound easier than it is. We've all been drawn to people who aren't good for us or have been overly angry from time to time, so it takes practice—sometimes lots of practice—to break the patterns that allow us to enter into these negative situations. To get good at exercising this sort of discipline and willpower over the big things in your life, maybe start small, like by denying yourself dessert once in a while, or forcing yourself to spend a little extra time studying rather than watching TV before bed. Eventually you'll be able to implement these Truths in all kinds of situations.

To give you just a little bit more practice working with these Truths, I'm going to take you through two final sections. The first section requires only that you see how one of my former patients, Anastasia, used the Ten Truths to deal with some issues that were impacting her life. The second offers you some final opportunities to practice using the Ten Truths in your own life.

Analyzing Anastasia

Anastasia is 17 years old and in her junior year of high school. In many ways she is a typical teen. She works hard to maintain a high GPA in school, plays goalie for their undefeated field hockey team, and volunteers several hours each Saturday cleaning animal cages at the local pet shelter. She and her boyfriend Miguel have been together for two years, and she has a small circle of close friends she has known since middle school. She lives with her mom and older brother Denny, who is 23, and she has an adorable little dog named Goober. Anastasia hopes to go to college after her senior year to double-major in veterinary sciences and business so one day she can own and operate her own veterinary clinic. Most days, Anastasia is friendly, considerate, and kind. All smiles, a really great kid.

Of course, life is not perfect for anyone, and Anastasia is no different. When Anastasia was 12 and her brother was 18 and just a few weeks away from graduating high school, Anastasia's dad revealed that he had been cheating on Anastasia's mom—with her best friend. Her parents soon divorced, and her dad moved out to live with his new girlfriend. For the first two years, Anastasia saw her dad on a regular basis—weekly at first, then only once or twice per month—but over the past three years she's barely seen him at all. He and his new wife have a child together—Anastasia's half-brother Graham—and since then he's barely come around to see Anastasia and Denny at all. A few months back Anastasia's grades began to slip. Several times last quarter she skipped school and field hockey practice to stay in bed all day. As a result, she missed a couple important quizzes that she never made up, sinking her grade, and she lost her role as starting goalie. Though she hadn't been spending as much time with her friends, especially her best friend Nia, she was still seeing her boyfriend Miguel almost every day. But last summer she began checking his phone when he used the bathroom or took the trash outside, and once she angrily accused him of cheating on her without any proof. Of course, this caused a real rift in their otherwise solid relationship, and it has caused a tension between them ever since. This was not her typical behavior.

Things weren't looking too great for Denny either. He quit college after his junior year and has been getting drunk several times per week for the past year. Three months ago, he was arrested for DUI and possession of a small amount of narcotics, and his lawyer says he might be facing up to 90 days in jail. Of course, this was a real concern for Anastasia. To make matters worse, Goober was recently diagnosed with inoperable brain cancer. The veterinarian told Anastasia she had two choices: put Goober down soon, or watch him die a slow, painful death at home. Faced with the impending loss of her childhood pet, Anastasia began to question whether she would ever have the strength to do the emotionally painful work required of a veterinarian, something she had wanted to be since she was a little girl.

After watching her children slowly slip away from her, and having a hard time herself since the divorce, Anastasia's mom reached out to a guidance counselor at Anastasia's school to get her daughter some help. After a meeting with her mom, counselor, and several of her teachers, Anastasia agreed to speak with a therapist once a week. Over the course of several months, I taught Anastasia the Ten Truths I have discussed in this book. Let's see how each of them helped Anastasia work through the issues in her life and get herself back on track. Let's see that Black Belt in action.

You Don't Have to be Confused by Your Feelings Anymore

For Anastasia, this first Truth was like a game of connect-the-dots. Because she had always been such a high functioning and happy person, Anastasia's low feelings were confusing to her. She knew she had been feeling down lately, and she knew she had been letting some things—like school, field hockey, and her friends, for example—slip, but she hadn't quite figured out why. She had begun to think that maybe a little sad and sluggish is just the way she is sometimes. After a couple sessions, though, Anastasia began to realize that her recent changes in mood and performance didn't just happen for no reason; she was mildly depressed. And for understandable reasons—her parents' divorce, her estrangement from her father, her brother's troubles, school, Goober. In fact, I told Anastasia that I would have been more concerned with her if she *hadn't* been feeling a little down lately. With all that she had been going through, it was only natural for her to want to spend some days hiding under the covers. Once Anastasia realized that her feelings had causes—and that she had control over how she reacted to them—she began to look at her emotional situation less as something permanent and confusing and more as something temporary and manageable.

You Can Control Your Compulsive Behaviors if You Change Your Thoughts and Address Your Problems

Luckily for Anastasia, she never developed any problematic behaviors. She doesn't drink, smoke, or use drugs. She doesn't steal, cut herself, or engage in any other risky behaviors. She does—I mean, *did*—have one compulsive behavior, however: she let herself get down far too often, and it began to impact her life. After going through so many difficult times over the past few years—but especially in the past few months—Anastasia began to adopt a defeatist attitude, meaning her thinking became so negative that she started to *expect* things to be bad. In some cases—like her reaction to a disagreement with a teacher over an essay that needed to be revised—Anastasia's pessimistic attitude created small emotional mountains when there might otherwise have been only molehills. As soon as something—anything—began to look a little challenging or difficult, Anastasia withdrew from the situation until she eventually began to withdraw almost completely. If not caught early, this compulsive negative thinking had the potential to become a full-blown habit, and like any other habit—drugs, excessive cell phone usage, gambling—it could have been difficult to break. When Anastasia began to realize that compulsive pessimism was becoming a problem in her life, she began to look for its signs and triggers and to give herself little pep talks to get back on her feet.

Every Behavior Has a Purpose (and It's Not Always What You Think)

One of the issues that was causing unnecessary pain for Anastasia was her suspicion that her boyfriend Miguel was cheating on her and the arguments that ensued when she accused him without any proof. When we first met, Anastasia insisted that she had a right to be suspicious of Miguel because, a few months before, after an evening of sitting with Anastasia while she alternated between tears and silence, Miguel told her he was going home to do some homework. Instead, he went to the mall with his friends—including a few girls—and ran into Anastasia's friend Gina who told Anastasia right away that she had seen him. When Anastasia accused Miguel not only of lying, but of cheating too, he told her that her crying and silence had been stressing him out and that he needed to get out of the house without hurting her feelings even more. He insisted, however, that he had never cheated.

When I asked Anastasia why she was so hung up on accusing Miguel of cheating—even going as far as to invade the privacy of his cell phone—she said his lie made him untrustworthy. I told Anastasia that everyone—including her—lies on occasion and that, while it was wrong of Miguel to lie, he did it so he wouldn't hurt her feelings about needing to have some space that night. Anastasia admitted that deep down she knew this to be true, but still she felt the need to snoop and accuse. Why, then? Well, the answer seems obvious now, but at the time Anastasia wasn't ready to confront the real reason for her behavior: Watching her father cheat on her mother had impacted her deeply and made her mistrustful of someone who wasn't untrustworthy. Anastasia apologized to Miguel for accusing him of cheating, and he apologized for not being totally honest with her. Since then, they have been much more open with one another, and Anastasia has come to realize that she should not allow *her father's* past misbehaviors to interfere with *her* relationship and emotional well being.

Sometimes Your Worst Enemy is *You*

In our first meeting, when I asked Anastasia why she thought she was unhappy, she blamed her sadness on her parents' divorce, her brother's recent troubles with substances and the law, and Goober's diagnosis. And let's be real: Who *wouldn't* be sad over these things? But when I asked her what was causing her to do poorly in school, to withdraw emotionally from her boyfriend and friends, and to begin to give up on her goals, her answer was the same. But there is a difference between a reason and an excuse, so while Anastasia's recent run of bad circumstances may have been a reason for her sadness and mild depression, it was not an excuse to simply give up and let the rest of her life be anything less than amazing. The truth of the matter was that Anastasia was allowing herself to be driven by fear—her inner saboteur telling her to avoid painful things—and this fear was keeping her from moving ahead with her life. She feared not having the support she felt she needed from her parents and her brother, so she stopped putting in the hard work at school. She feared abandonment and disloyalty, so she created unnecessary problems in her relationship with Miguel. And she feared the occasional emotional pain that is surely part of the life of a veterinarian, so she allowed herself to believe that it was no longer a goal worth pursuing.

Over time, Anastasia began to realize that fear, uncertainty about the future, and the actions of others are not legitimate reasons to be unhappy and to not pursue her dreams. Ultimately she began to see that the only thing standing between her and happiness was *herself.* Determined not to let the evil little voice of her inner saboteur tell her what to be afraid of and what to avoid, Anastasia began to take back the direction of her life and to embrace the challenges that lie ahead.

All Behavior Requires Permission, so You Must Learn What You're Permitting Yourself to Do

Once Anastasia discovered through Truth N°4 that a lot of her pain—the negative thinking, the self-sabotage— was self-induced, Truth N°5 came much more easily and was a real breakthrough for her. For example, Anastasia realized that she avoided school even more when she started getting lower grades, and, of course, that only made matters worse, not better. But no one *forced* her to skip, and no one *forced* her not to make up the quizzes or redo the writing assignment her teacher asked her to fix. Likewise, no one forced her to accuse Miguel of cheating when she had no evidence he was or to invade his privacy every time he left his phone unguarded. Anastasia gave herself *permission* to do these things. She realized that her actions were choices, that her choices have negative consequences, and that she can avoid the consequences by no longer choosing these actions. No longer willing to blame others for circumstances that are within her control, Anastasia accepted responsibility for her actions and began to reclaim control over her behavior.

You Have a Limited Amount of Emotional Energy, so It Shouldn't be Wasted on Wishing, Worrying, and Whining

Since for most of her life Anastasia had been so focused and goal-oriented, she understood fully how valuable her time is. Earning good grades, improving at field hockey, volunteering, and maintaining healthy relationships do not allow for too much wasted time. But a major negative shift occurred when she allowed those three ugly Ws to creep into her life. She *wished* her parents hadn't divorced, that her dad came around more often, and that Denny hadn't gotten mixed up with drugs and alcohol. She *worried* that Miguel was cheating on her, that Denny might go to jail, and that Goober was suffering. And she *whined* about how much homework she was receiving in her advanced classes, about how many hours she had to spend at field hockey practice, and about how much poop she had to clean up at the pet shelter. Eventually she wished, worried, and whined so much about these things that she didn't have any time to actually *do* them. When Anastasia realized that her negative attitude wouldn't actually change anything—for example, she could never wish her parents back together, worry her brother out of a jail sentence, or whine her way to a better grade—she decided to adjust her way of thinking. This does not mean she no longer has concerns; it simply means she doesn't allow herself to waste time stressing over things she can't control. Instead, she controls what she can and lets the rest happen on its own. As a result, she feels a great deal of anxiety lifted off of her shoulders, and she is much more proactive and productive than she ever had been.

Healthy Relationships Depend on Self-Empowerment, Not on Trying to Fix Others

Anastasia's relationship with her brother Denny had always been particularly strong, but they grew even closer in the years following their parents' divorce because they had a shared pain and relied on each other for emotional support. Naturally, Anastasia would do just about anything for her brother, but his turn to drugs and alcohol put an emotional strain on her. Sometimes Anastasia would pick him up from parties if he was too drunk to drive, or she would lie to her mom that he wasn't feeling well to cover for the times he was too hungover to get out of bed. In the beginning, these things happened only occasionally, but over time this enabling behavior became much more frequent. Anastasia was dealing with her own grief in her own way, but trying to fix her older brother became more than she could handle. When Denny was arrested, Anastasia blamed herself, claiming that if she had charged her phone that night, she would have received his text about needing a ride, and he wouldn't have ended up driving drunk. On top of everything else she was dealing with, she carried the unnecessary guilt for his arrest.

In therapy, Anastasia came to realize that, just like she was giving herself permission for certain behaviors, so too was Denny giving himself permission to use drugs and drink and drive. She realized that he owns his behaviors and that she is not responsible for him. Yes, it is natural for her to want the best for her brother and for her to help when she can, but a healthy relationship between siblings does not include the teenage sister constantly cleaning up the messes of the adult brother. Eventually Anastasia understood that Denny needed help, but she was not the one qualified to give it to him. She also came to understand that by lying for him and picking him up from parties she was, in fact, making his problems worse, not better. Anastasia told Denny that she would no longer cover for him if he continued to drink and use drugs, but she promised him that she would always be there to support him in his recovery. With the heavy burden of caring for her big brother off her shoulders, Anastasia was better prepared to work on her own emotional recovery.

TRUTH N°8

Ego Boundaries Protect Us from Rejection, Insult, and Intimidation

As many young people do, Anastasia took the divorce of her parents very personally. Because her parents often argued about "the kids," Anastasia developed the misguided belief that their divorce was her fault. Her suspicions grew when her dad started coming by to see her less and less frequently, and she was absolutely convinced that she was the world's worst daughter and the sole cause of her parents' unhappiness when he stopped calling almost entirely. Though it took some time, Anastasia eventually began to see that her dad's actions—or inactions, to be more precise—were a reflection that he was failing in *his* duties, not that she was failing in hers. She began to realize that she was not responsible for making her dad come around; she was responsible only for herself—for being a good daughter to her mother and a good role model for her baby brother, even though she saw him rarely. Using Truth N°8, Anastasia was able to create a necessary boundary between her father's behaviors and her emotional responses to them.

You Can Trust People to be Who They Are, Not Who You Want Them to Be

Among the several issues that were bringing Anastasia down was her relationship with Nia, her best friend since middle school. When I asked what made Nia her best friend, Anastasia told me that Nia was the first person to make her feel welcome at her new school when she moved from out of town in sixth grade. Nia introduced her to a small group of friends, and they had been hanging out ever since. But Nia wasn't always such a good friend. She had a tendency to make fun of Anastasia in front of other people, to spread untrue rumors about her, and to make plans and cancel them at the last minute. Recently Nia flirted with Miguel at a party, and when Anastasia confronted her about it, Nia actually pushed her to the ground and laughed at her. The worst part, though, was that no matter how badly Nia acted toward Anastasia, she always made *Anastasia* apologize to *her* before she allowed her back into their circle of friends.

When I asked Anastasia why she tolerated such behavior from her so-called friend, her only reply was that Nia was there for her when she didn't know anyone in middle school. I explained that, while it was very kind for Nia to be so welcoming to the new girl, this didn't give her the right to abuse her for the next five years. Anastasia admitted that she had always known her relationship with Nia was toxic, but she felt a certain loyalty to her, and deep down she always hoped Nia would change and become a better friend—the kind of friend Anastasia was to her. Truth N°9 helped Anastasia realize that her relationship with Nia had given her a lot more pain and social anxiety than it had given her actual friendship and support. She admitted she had seen Nia act this way with others, too, and that she showed no signs of changing—in fact, she had been getting worse over time. Over several weeks of therapy, Anastasia came to realize that she

CONCLUSION

didn't need nasty Nia in her life anymore, and she felt a great deal of relief when she let their friendship finally come to its natural and necessary end.

Time Doesn't Heal All Pain; We Heal Ourselves by Learning to Let Pain Go

Several weeks into our sessions together, Anastasia made the difficult decision to put down her dog Goober. She delayed the awful day for as long as she could, but there came a point when she could see that the cancer was causing him serious pain, and she made the right decision to put him to rest painlessly. Luckily, Anastasia had been seeing me before she made this decision, so she was able to prepare emotionally for it in advance. This preparation didn't make the sad day any easier, but it gave her a solid foundation to begin the healing process when it was over.

With my help, Anastasia used the five-step process in Truth N°10 to help her prepare for and process Goober's death. When she shared with me several photos and fond memories of Goober, I encouraged her to be open with her feelings—not to ignore them or try to hold them back—so you can imagine there were both lots of laughter over his goofy antics and lots of tears over the pain of his death. Then Anastasia found several productive ways to honor Goober's memory. She made a scrapbook of photos of the two of them together, and a few weeks later, she began to volunteer *more* at the local pet shelter, admitting that, while she still felt pretty sad about his passing, spending time around other dogs just made her feel really good inside. Most importantly, though, Anastasia realized that running away from her career goal of becoming a veterinarian just to avoid the occasional pain it was sure to cause was no way to honor Goober's memory or to live her life. Instead, she determined to use her own experience as a source of strength to help her save as many sick animals as she could and to help their owners deal with their losses whenever those sad times came.

I am so proud of Anastasia. She turned her pain into strength, resiliency, and purpose—a true Social Black Belt if I ever saw one.

You're Almost There!

Now that you've seen how Anastasia used the Ten Truths to earn her Social Black Belt, all that remains is for you to do the same. Applying these Truths isn't simple, but it's not particularly hard either. All it takes is practice—lots of practice. The exercises at the end of each chapter were designed to help you get started. These final exercises will help you maintain the routine.

TRUTH N°1

Try to identify an emotion you sometimes feel without knowing why. It can be sadness, anger, anxiety, or anything else that bothers you. Write the emotion in the circle below. Then, at the end of the arrows, write what situations or events cause this emotion. For example, maybe your emotion is fear, and one of the causes is being left home alone at night while your parents go out with their friends. Once you identify the causes of your feelings, address them using some of the other Ten Truths.

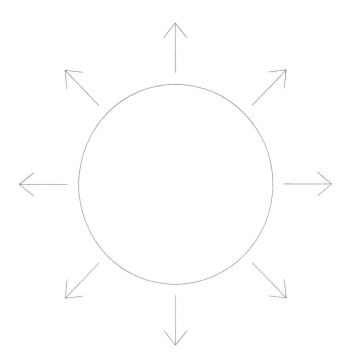

TRUTH N°2

Now that you've identified a negative feeling and some of its causes, think about how you've dealt with this feeling in the past. For this exercise, write a simple "Before" and "After" statement describing how you handled this feeling in the past and how you'll handle it now that you've learned this Truth. For example, "Before, when I felt overwhelmed about my homework, I avoided it and played video games all night. After I learned Truth N°2, I realized that avoiding the work doesn't make it going away. Now I make a schedule and manage my time better." Keep this Truth in mind when you find your negative feelings causing negative behaviors. Then allow yourself to move in a positive direction.

Before_____

_____

_____

_____

_____

After_____

_____

_____

_____

_____

TRUTH N°3

Try to identify your most mysterious compulsive behavior—the one you do over and over again even though you know it's bad for you. Is it vaping? Obsessive eating? Shoplifting? Now think about what you think you accomplish with this behavior. Does it make you feel cool, or does it numb your pain? Does it give you a rush of adrenaline? Now, identify other, healthier ways you can recreate that same feeling. For example, wouldn't it also feel cool to learn how to play the guitar? Wouldn't you also feel a rush by taking up boxing or going for a run in the park? Once you've identified what's bad for you and why you do it, continue working on these healthy alternatives to get you through your troubled times.

Compulsive Behavior

_____

_____

What You Hope to Accomplish

_____

_____

_____

Healthy Alternatives

1. _____

2. _____

3. _____

Think about a time when your inner saboteur has talked you out of a goal, like auditioning for the school play or asking for a raise at your job. Draw a picture of this hideous monster, including some of the negative things it tries to convince you of that aren't true. For example, does it tell you you're not good enough to get the lead role or not smart enough to deserve that raise? Then, draw yourself and write a few lines of dialogue you can tell your saboteur—in other words, yourself—that will help you move past these crippling fears and toward your goals.

TRUTH N°5

Create a list of several negative behaviors you give yourself permission to do. Do you give yourself permission to
lie to your parents, cheat on your homework, or spread
rumors about people on social media? Then write *why*
you have given yourself permission to do these things.
Do you want to avoid being grounded, or failing a class?
Does it make you feel better about yourself to spread
rumors or see others be hurt? Finally, now that you've
identified these behaviors and the excuses you've made
up for giving yourself permission to do them, identify the
opposite, positive actions you will give yourself permission to do so you can get the same reaction. For example,
maybe you will stop doing the thing that might get you
grounded, dedicate a little time to homework and studying, or make friends with people instead of bringing
them down.

Bad Behaviors You Give Yourself Permission to Do

1. _____

2. _____

3. _____

New Behaviors You Will Permit Yourself to Do Instead

1. _____

2. _____

3. _____

TRUTH N°6

It's time to think about all the ways you waste time wishing, worrying, and whining. On any given day, write an X in the box every time you find yourself wishing something were different than it is, worrying about something you have no control over, or whining about something you can fix. At the end of the day, count your Xs to determine how much time and emotional energy you wasted that day. The next day, do the same thing, but use yesterday's log as a reminder that your time and emotional energy are precious. Make a decision to rededicate all that wasted time on things that you are passionate about and will benefit you, like fixing a problem, pursuing a goal, improving a relationship, or practicing a hobby. After you've spent a few days focusing on changing your thought patterns, try the Xs activity again to see if you have a lower count. Continue as needed until you see results you're satisfied with.

DAY 1		TOTAL
DAY 2		TOTAL
DAY 3		TOTAL

TRUTH N°7

Identify the person in your life who has the biggest impact on your mood. Before seeing or speaking to that person, remind yourself that he or she does not have the power to control your happiness. Repeat to yourself, "(Name) cannot, should not, and will not determine my mood today. I am strong on my own, and my happiness comes from within." To help you get used to thinking this way, write that internal dialogue three times on the lines below. Feel free to create your own as well. Remember, while it is perfectly acceptable to try to help people you love, you are no one's doormat. You must empower yourself before you can help other people. This is one of the keys to healthy relationships.

1. _____

_____

_____

2. _____

_____

_____

3. _____

_____

_____

TRUTH N°8

Now it's time to draw your boundaries—literally. On the left, write the names of people and descriptions of how they reject, insult, or intimidate you, as well as what this says about them. For example, you might write, "Tony makes fun of me in class because he is trying to impress his friends." Seeing these boundaries should remind you that what others do and say reflects on them, not on you. Then, on the other side, describe the people who you know are always looking out for your best interests—in other words the people you feel safe allowing inside your boundaries. You might write, "Svetlana always offers me great advice when I'm feeling down about myself." This should remind you of who to trust and who to look for when you're in need of a friend.

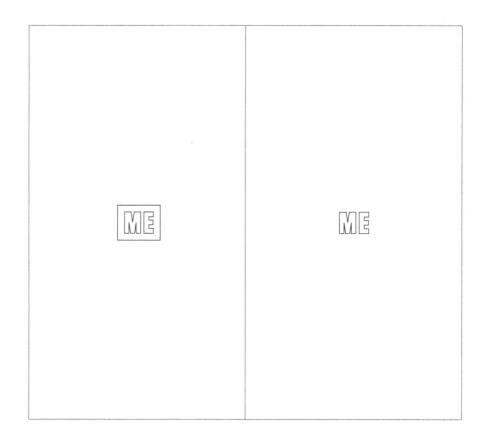

TRUTH N°9

Think about the person in your life who most frequently lets you down. Identify what you have expected of them that they have not been able to fulfil, and try to determine what it is about them—something in their past, perhaps—that prevents them from living up to your expectations. Finally, given what you know about their past behaviors, try to set new expectations of them going forward. If you are realistic about how this person is likely to behave, you will be less disappointed in the future. This does not mean you should not have high expectations of people—but you should have realistic ones. Remember: You can control only yourself. Don't allow yourself to be weighed down by the failures of others.

Name

Old Expectations

New Expectations

TRUTH N°10

Think of a past experience or trauma that still causes you emotional pain. Then think of someone you trust—a family member, close friend, teacher, therapist, or religious leader—and ask them to help you through the five steps of healing: remembering, feeling, expressing, releasing, and changing thinking. Just as you would seek out the aid of a doctor to fix a broken arm, you must seek out the help of someone you trust to help you heal your inner wounds. Finally, think of 3-5 fun and healthy activities you can engage in to help you push through the hard times. What's most important here is that you will not be passive and just expect things to get better eventually. You must take an active role in your emotional health.

Event That Still Causes Pain

_____

Person I Can Talk To

_____

Healthy Activities for Healing

1. _____

2. _____

3. _____

4. _____

5. _____

And Finally, the Truth About the Social Black Belt

Just as time doesn't heal all wounds, simply having read *The Social Black Belt* will not magically cure your addictions, lift your depression, give you wings to be a social butterfly, or turn you from a D student to an A student overnight. What it has done, hopefully, is to provide you with a better understanding of yourself so you can— gradually, over time, and with constant practice—become the better version of yourself you know you are capable of becoming.

Understanding how your mind works is the key to understanding why you think, feel, and behave the way you do. Your mind is your greatest tool, and, like any complex tool, the more you are aware of its functions and capabilities, the more control you will have over it. The more control you have over your mind, the better you will be able to use it to your maximum advantage, and the less you will find yourself thinking, feeling, or acting in ways you don't understand or can't manage.

It is important to understand that this book is not a substitute for therapy, so if you feel you need professional help, you should talk to a trusted adult to seek counseling. But for everyday issues like relationships, school, or simply managing your emotions, it is exactly what's needed. At first, working these Ten Truths may take some getting used to, but like most things you practice for a long time, they will eventually feel natural to you. And that's the thing about a Social Black Belt: Just a like a martial arts black belt, once you earn it, you have to *continue* to earn it. But don't worry, the destination is *definitely* worth the journey. If you continue to travel the road to a happier, healthier, and better you, using these Ten Truths as your guide, you will reach a point when you no longer *wear* a Social Black Belt: you will *be* one. Now that's what I call kickin' butt.

ABOUT THE AUTHORS

Dr. Christopher Cortman is a licensed psychologist with over 35 years and 75,000 hours of facilitating psychotherapy. He is the author of four books about mental health, including *Your Mind: An Owner's Manual for a Better Life: 10 Simple Truths That Will Set You Free; Take Control of Your Anxiety;* and *Keep Pain in the Past: Getting Over Trauma, Grief and the Worst Thing That's Ever Happened to You.* In addition to his role as private practitioner and on-call psychologist for Venice Regional Bayfront Health, Dr. Cortman serves as founder and director of The Social Black Belt, a program aimed at developing social, emotional, and behavioral awareness in people of all ages, particularly children and adolescents. The Social Black Belt is a proud partner of the NFL Alumni Association.

Using his unique blend of expertise and wit, Dr. Cortman has engaged audiences on nationally recognized television and radio programs, including on Disney Radio, MTV, and ABC, and he has used his respected voice to speak on issues of mental health alongside the likes of Tipper Gore, Jane Pauley, and Patrick Kennedy.

For his efforts, Dr. Cortman was awarded the Reader's Choice Award for Best Psychologist by the Venice

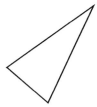

Gondolier Sun for six consecutive years (2013-2018) and the award for Outstanding Contributions to Psychology in the Public Interest by the Florida Psychological Association in 2015.

The proud father of three chronically unemployed children, all under the age of fourteen, Dr. Cortman lives with his partner in Sarasota, Florida.

———

Born in New Jersey and raised in Pennsylvania, **Michael Keelen** has lived in Sarasota, Florida, for over 20 years. A former at-risk youth, Mr. Keelen has volunteered for numerous charitable organizations, coached youth sports, and directed a mentorship program for at-risk adolescents. Holding three degrees from the University of South Florida system, including a Master of Arts in English Education, he has been teaching high school English in Florida's public school system since 2014. In his spare time, he enjoys reading, traveling, and drinking lots of tea. He has one son. This is his first book.